The Last Jubilee

EndofdaysBooks.com

By JR Hyat

DEDICATION

This work is dedicated in the servitude of His Spirit, completed on the 40th day through Elul to Yom Kippur, for a testimony of His guiding hand. However, one chart was added 10 days prior to the 47th election in the final chapter as the Word came as it always has every 4 years.

Copyright © 2024, DBA JR Hyat. The author guarantees all contents are original and do not infringe upon the legal rights of any other person or work. No part of this book may be reproduced in any form without the permission of the author. Due to the changing nature of the Internet, if there are any web addresses, links, or URLs included in this manuscript, these may have been altered and may no longer be accessible. All Scripture quoted is the King James Version (KJV), published 1769; Public Domain, unless otherwise noted. ISBN: 9798345778289

INTRODUCTION	6
1. BRIDGE OVER TROUBLE WATERS II	8
2. THE BEGINNING AND BEYOND	26
3. AGE TO AGE	39
4. LET THE FEAST BEGIN	49
5. A FEAST TO REMEMBER	61
6. WHAT A DIFFERENCE A DAY MAKES	77
7. NOT IN MY TOWN	96
8. 8 IS ENOUGH	111
9. SAVING THE WORLD	124
10 THE U.S. IN HEBREW HISTORY	137
11. PARTING WAYS	150
12. SMOKE OR MIRRORS	168
13. MONSTERS OR MYTHS	185
14. LOVE AND IDEOLOGY	201
16. ILLUSIONS AND ILLUSTRATIONS	212
17. JUST THE ESSENTIALS	222

INTRODUCTION

This book takes a fact-based journey facing the realization that the end of an Age is imminent. The quest analyzes society, the Old Testament festivals, Christianity, probabilities, and reason. By the conclusion of chapter 17, it becomes statistically undeniable that we are living in the final days before destruction.

Likewise, it has confounded me how Jewish leaders missed the return of the Messiah when given prophecy indicating Yeshua's birth. This same thought process resurfaces in the concept of a second coming of Jesus for the Christian faith. These personal observations have pushed me toward the seemingly impossible task of investigating the probabilities as to the season of Christ's return. Because of a few verses taken out of context, the Christian faith has neglected to fully probe the notion that we are in the same boat as the first-century Jew. Just as the Jews overlooked the first coming of Christ, most Christians will miss His 2nd return. This is due to several factors, some of which are discussed within the confines of this book.

Unfortunately, predominantly all of the Christian faith has claimed ignorance of divine messages meant to forewarn civilization of a coming cataclysmic event. Let me be clear, while the faith agrees in a final battle they call Armageddon, they have essentially worn blinders about prophecies concerning the season of Yeshua's return. This lack of scriptural focus has become rampant and excusable within the religious hierarchy. This book examines some trappings along this road toward Truth to enhance an ongoing quest focused on the end of days. Bluntly, these snares are self-imposed mostly because the body of believers have become inoculated to religion as a whole or have accepted handed-down beliefs without diligently searching scripture for themselves. Some of these pitfalls are shocking. Some remain relatively unnoticed. Other trappings are vehemently defended doctrines embedded within decades of seminary walls if not longer.

As for this book, much of it encompassed sporadic spurts of writing. Sometimes that infrequent nature looked like a paragraph over one-week, other times five to ten pages the following week. In between, there were large breaks involving prayer, patience, and listening. This was the first time in my writing career that such wide and varied gaps existed. Had my other duties not been so distracting at times those intervals may have been more unsettling. Sure, there were periods of research and reading as in prior books, but these types of pauses were unusually different. These were periods of patience while waiting upon the Lord. Every notion of what to write next became an indefinite waiting game. The urgency to finish still existed, yet there was no anxiety to set out before the Spirit. Certainly, this manifested as a direct result of a change in prayer life that gradually progressed over the previous years. As a result, prayer would produce the most revealing book in the series. Once finished, the message was clear. But would it register with the average person? Who would accept it if the entire religious system pushed against it? Would it make a difference? Answering these types of questions wasn't up to me. So, I persevered, not knowing the results but embracing the Truth as prescribed to me. More answers are now available for those who have an ear. Let them pray to hear.

BRIDE OVER TROUBLED WATERS II

I walked into my dream last night. Entering the main conference room were seated the usual teachers. Everyone was there just as they had been years earlier. The guidance counselor was shuffling her papers preparing herself before the meeting was to begin. Sherri was seated closest to the door with her back to me as I entered the room. My only thought was to stop directly beside the table and give her a big two-armed side hug while she remained seated. She responded in like fashion. I whispered in her ear as we embraced, "I know you're not really here." That is to say, the scenario itself was staged.

As our loving embrace released, I observed the gazes from the other teachers seated around the oval conference table. They did not see what I saw. Their facial expressions only confirmed what I already knew. This was not a meeting intended for them. It was a personal farewell from the heart. Their displeasure or favor didn't matter in the least. I had outgrown the need for the approval of peers. In that instant, Sherri vanished from the scene, no longer visible to me yet her presence remained forever ingrained within my heart. Cherishing the thought, I reminisced how Sherri had been a casualty of COVID-19 only months beforehand. That was the moment I awoke sobbing. Wiping away the tears, somehow, I knew this was not just a normal dream, but a gift.

Searching for meaning, I decidedly inquired as to why this occurred. Was it merely zealous speculation? If it was heaven-sent there had to be a purpose. The pursuit for an answer enacted an instantaneous response. Immediately, it was brought to memory that I was not informed about her illness. I was barely notified about her funeral arrangements in time to attend. Truthfully, I was grateful to have been notified at all. In my consciousness, this nullified the idea of harboring any resentment. Or could it be that deep within my subconscious remained a mixture of bitterness? Who knows what sort of psychiatric complexity our minds invent as coping mechanisms... Some may suggest that whether the nature of the vision was self-imposed or divinely inspired makes little difference when viewed through a prism of healthy outcomes. There is little argument that healing comes in many forms whether mentally or physically, consciously or subconsciously. Was it even so important to know why the dream occurred? And why did several months pass until the conference room get together? Apparently, on some level, it was important to me. Reinforced during the writing of my previous book, Seer in the Way, it has become increasingly clear that nothing occurs in a vacuum. So, if the dream, or vision, was heaven-sent there must be a reason. Leaning into this truth, straightaway the veil was lifted. Indeed, this was a divinely sanctioned encounter, verified as Sherri remained legitimately present in my vision. The supporting cast members were an illusion to prove a second point. The second point was a marker on the milestone of progress I'd made regarding how past feelings of inferiority had negatively affected my performance. Previously, my poor self-perception often created obstacles preventing me from excelling in my everyday life. So, it's not that other people's opinions never matter, moreover, those interjections curbed my confidence from asserting certain Truths from taking a rightful leadership role in my life. Acting on what I know to be true no longer required anyone's approval. So, whether or not other teachers acknowledged the event as real didn't matter. In the end, this was a personal gift meant solely for me. It was my moment to express love for a cherished friend. It was my moment to express goodbyes given divinely by a higher supernatural friend. This gift I will remember and treasure into the next realm, forever.

Recognizing there is often a bigger purpose, I looked beyond myself and inquired for a grander question. Years earlier such questions could easily have been glossed over or overlooked entirely. Yet, in the past two years, it has become glaringly apparent that individual perceptions have long imprisoned our insights affecting how things are interpreted. Even worse, our degree of selfishness interferes with our ability to analyze and overcome the simplest of circumstances. For example, had I concluded this was just a bad dream or just about me, the scenario would have remained contained, diluted, or even forgotten in short order. However, recent experiences have taught me to ask questions about the spiritual and parse what is real from fictitious. This requires a direct query, a conscious act of will. It is spawned from life's experiences and sometimes by direct revelation. Moreover, sound inquiry requires relevant questions. Oddly still, the best questions I have ever asked came as a reply to my original inquiry. As it were, a question with a question. In these instances, it is logical to re-ask the request or at least ponder both. Slowly repeating the initial question forces me to focus and not alter it in any way. This managed behavior helps to minimize the probability of misunderstanding, underestimating, or overestimating the gravity of the outcome. This may sound convoluted to some or like a logical progression of thoughts to others, however amid emotional turmoil it is often difficult to stay grounded and act rationally. Most assuredly, after my vision and heartfelt tears for Sherri subsided it was more miraculous to rebound rationally by asking pragmatic questions. But this process was essential in unpacking and understanding the bigger picture. That bigger picture was, and is, wrapped in the value of building confidence for the whole body. Let's unwrap several steps and see the grand prize.

Already addressed is the notion of overcoming preconceived misconceptions of reality and doctrine. This invented hurdle is often the first snare preventing many from merely entering the race. Avoiding this requires serious self-reflection and the removal of false teachings most never think are incorrect in the first place. In many cases the race never began or if it ever did the time was long ago and never reconsidered. Thus, those religious ideologies are often never replaced and the status quo rests firmly intact. The severity of this inaction prevents the noticeable progression of personal evolution. This insidious avoidance frequently masks itself as growth. That stream of consciousness sets adrift all who are willingly misled or stagnant. Concealed are the obstacles of a self-imposed roadblock that hinders future growth and all its benefits. The type of roadblock only permits a surface-level action because the basic root issues or questions are never truly assessed. Scripture refers to this layer of consciousness as an underwater sea creature, Leviathan. This is a safe but shallow existence. This surface-level existence gives the drifter an illusion of justification for his actions generally displayed with a controlling attitude that compels them to be frequently "right." Still, others stay secure in their ignorance contesting nothing. In either instance, it does not equate to living life more abundantly.

Self-reflection is difficult because it suggests the possibility that we are wrong. Typically, people don't like to be corrected. Perhaps it is because they don't like to apologize or ask forgiveness. Modern lingo twists correction negatively in the colloquial of judging others. However, closer examination reveals that if people never humbly ask the most pertinent required questions to help themselves, how can anyone become acutely effective in helping others? If we ever were helpful to others, this type of snare would eventually grow countless weeds and thorns choking out all future fruits we could be embracing. Therefore, we should examine ourselves, not just for ourselves, but for our loved ones. Furthermore, professing our love for one another requires an obligation of demonstration. This demonstration should be a visible act of consistent care and discipline in faith. Love is not just an emotion; love is faith in action.

Love cannot be produced by avoiding good relationships, though many people consistently try. Ironically, many who are avoiding good relationships appear to seek them. They marry and have families just like everyone else. These people live a surface life of "love" never fully committed to anything but themselves. They live running from a deeper spiritual commitment, never facing the questions they know must be asked of themselves. Sometimes they are sad and sometimes they lash out in anger or both. They remain largely unsatisfied their entire life. This is exhibited by who they choose as spouses, and how they treat others. Weirdly, relationship avoidance often fosters a false sense of control. Control is a false substitute for love commonly found in many unhealthy relationships. So many today will never admit that they are control freaks hiding behind a misguided concept of love. Of course, most people would never admit to being domineering. Nor will they ask for your opinion.

Ultimately, avoidance is the Leviathan factor preventing believers from drawing a favorable conclusion concerning dreams and revelations. Avoidance is usually parsed with the religious dogma of disbelief, heresy, or the notion that all sorts of Christian acts or ideals died with the Apostles centuries ago. This frontal attack is designed to eliminate any retort about modern miracle healings or revelation; it also ensnares the weaker believer into a lifeless abundance. These people denounce vision and redefine it. Thus, all clinging to this ideology fundamentally disable themselves. Their outcomes are limited by the lack of revelation predetermined by their unwillingness to inquire beyond the boundaries of man's limitations. This phenomenon is by no means new. The Jewish interaction with Yeshua at the beginning of the new age produced a similar response. A Christian Jesus simply didn't fit in the box previously built by religious leaders of that day. Today, this is expressed more vividly and perhaps more harshly by the idea that religious leaders continually interpret scripture differently. This generally occurs when our interpretation of God's divine plans supplants true spiritual application. The fitting example of this division arrives in the form of countless denominations all claiming to have the one "right" view of scripture. The truth is that none of them are 100% correct.

The takeaway is that rectifying false faith can be a perilous adventure not for the faint at heart. For leaders, most would have a difficult time coming to grips with reinventing themselves should they differ from the prescribed dogma. Besides, denominational leadership doesn't always take a kind view of those departing from traditional ideals. Certain foundational lines are drawn at the beginning of seminary training and are the most difficult to correct, especially if leadership doesn't believe something needs correction. This has been true for centuries. Understanding this history, it makes sense why it seems easier for so many clergy to stay on their current trajectory, saving face, and avoiding what would become personal embarrassment at the very least. Perhaps this is the reason why Jesus chose the uneducated 12. Jesus embraced their hearts, not their education. He rejected the prideful nature of the establishment. Pride hides itself deeply beneath avoidance. The result of clinging to various illogical attributes brings the horror that avoidance is denial and denial embraces pride. Few will likely admit to any error that subjects themselves to such a psychological house of cards. They are immersed in a sea of Leviathan. In this way, a lack of humility easily ensnares entire groups and congregations. It is the most popular plague of our age as evidenced by the Sermon on the Mount. Even the idea of dying to self for the will of God has been corrupted with promises of prosperity and healing.

Confronted with these issues, it becomes evident that any notion of meekness as a virtue has been highjacked. This plague has produced stunted growth and unnecessary division within the body of believers. The cure is constant prayerful introspection, extending reason and grace toward one another. This is the command of Christ, to be one as Christ and the Father are one. This is not to suggest that we come together embracing clearly defined issues of heresy. Adopting abominations will inevitably lead to destruction.

God forbid any believer is left behind on that final day. Nor should the church turn on itself. Remember the story of Saul. He exhibited great zeal by endorsing the scripture to the point of executing Christians. The religious establishment of that day considered his efforts worthy, accurate, and necessary to preserve the faith. Saul counted his actions as a duty and a favor for God. While Saul may have thought it was a clear depiction of carrying out the letter of the law he was illustrating a lack of spiritual application. Moreover, Saul relishes his position as a pharisee as well as his Jewish heritage until Jesus personally appears to change his mind. Paul is blinded as a sign to all just as the church today is blinded. Must history also dictate that the Christian church follow this trend to the end? Must we wait until another appearance before determining that we wear blinders within our denominational zeal? Or will His delayed arrival be misconstrued as confirmation that He may not appear at all?

Addressing this spiritual component, let us first agree that God's nature does not change; neither does God's nature hide, though it is invisible to those who do not believe or do not search with their whole heart. Hiding from the Truth is a fallen human reoccurrence. In other words, it is human nature to hide from God just as Adam & Eve exhibited in the Garden after identifying their own mistake. People have been hiding from God by inventing multitudes of unlimited excuses conjured up by the limited resources of fallible minds. Most can readily admit that Mankind indeed clothes itself in all sorts of self-absorbed notions such as money, work, spouses, children, etc. But doctrine is tricky. We normally point across the aisle to the other person's doctrine requiring adjustments. Nevertheless, many of these excusable endeavors can be viewed as good or bad depending on the perspectives applied to our everyday lives or culture. But regardless of man's vast array of ridiculous excuses and busy work environments, God is faithful to His word. God enjoys revealing His ways when approached with an honest open heart. There is no formula required. Come to prayer like a child.

On the other hand, some members of the Christian sect embrace the Holy Spirit as the Teacher of all revelation. Regrettably, many in this persuasion over-emphasize this thought process and profess that only God directly will lead them to all understanding. While God is always in complete control of all knowledge, the elect should be aware of the problems associated with strict adherence to such a limited interpretation of reality. If we examine this errant idea more closely, it should become apparent that this is another self-induced trap. Directly addressing this issue, I have observed a new trend of those who profess no need for biblical assistance in the search for scriptural Truth. While most correctly applaud individual search for understanding via the Holy Spirit, we have plenty of evidence that God is not restricted to one delivery method. The irony in this type of single delivery system is most disturbing. For example, why would someone ever need to ask a question to another individual if not to receive an answer? The speed of knowledge has equipped us to learn more quickly than ever before. In addition, God usually gives answers that are meant to be shared. Believers share scripture for the confidence and building of Faith. In the same way, if we disagree about a particular scripture, aren't we to reason together to arrive at the ultimate Truth? The body should seek to edify and enable one another. Must the entire body have the same function? Can't we accept there will be differences and focus on the message of the Godhead? Isn't the spiritual truth of salvation the only dividing line set forth by the Gospel's Good News? Each authentic party must return to this core message and exhibit honest exchanges from the position of potential fallibility. Discontinuing honest discussions by announcing "I'll only listen to God" or overtly stating "the scripture is the scripture" demeans all participants worthy of engagement aimed at the Truth. The definition of a body implies the notion that each denomination might disagree with certain functions and interpretations beyond that core belief of Good News. Furthermore, if we slander or condemn each other, we condemn ourselves, the bride of Christ and Christ. To suggest that there exists a single denomination that has all the answers correct or that professes every member believes exactly as every other demonstrates an overt action of pridefulness. Furthermore, the current argument of only using scripture breaks down since God has determined to use people to spread the Gospel 2 by 2. God certainly, uses preachers, disciples, prophets, apostles, animals, angels, dreams, visions, letters, books, weather, and events as a witness to the Truth. If not, why witness? Why go to church? The suggestion that God only uses Himself contradicts sending pilgrims to fulfill His purpose. God extends Himself through whatever vessel or device He chooses. This attitude is more likely to back us into a corner of pridefulness. Very few can proclaim as one voice crying in the wilderness.

If the elect becomes more cognizant that God uses the imperfect to glorify the perfect, grace will abound. Meekness and humility would play a natural transitionary role as believers regroup toward the core beliefs of the cross. This miracle power comes from the inside out. The Spirit of God transforms every praying believer demonstrating His mercy and grace. God does the impossible to prove His superior nature, the Truth. Anyone can use perfection to produce perfection. Only God can use a sin-riddled vessel to reflect the perfect Kingdom of righteousness. He molds imperfect people into His likeness as proof of the narrow Way. No one should usurp that divine kindness, grace, mercy, and love by exchanging it for pride, power, control, or denial. Christians should remember their role at the end of the day. Their pleasure will be to accept a symbolic participation trophy only to lay it at the feet of a deserving Messiah. A believer's birthright is the only gift for keeps. We marry into the rest.

Another error suggests that God only uses people to spread the Word of God. Preachers frequently imply their work as essential since faith comes by hearing the Word. This narrow-mindedness is self-serving and false. As explained, God can use many methods including presenting His Word personally as presented with Paul's interaction. Remember, Abraham had no scripture at all yet believed God. God can use a talking mule if He wants. The rocks would cry out if no one spoke the Truth. Man's vanity and limited thinking are deceitful. This causes spillover effects into man's conduct and scriptural interpretations. Therefore, our hearts are deceived when suggesting the foolishness of preaching is the only way to convert a soul into faith. The Truth is that everyone must individually receive God's rhema word on the tablets of their heart. This can only occur when spurred through the Spirit. Faith originates from the author. Thus, a believer neither introduces the Gospel nor escorts anyone into the Truth. Only the Spirit of God leads the Way. Every believer is merely permitted to participate. Remember, followers are dead to self, a vessel for the Spirit of God.

In reflection, it is a very narrow viewpoint that proposes God can only use certain methods we decide as the avenue for delivery. God is infinite. A man's finite understanding attempts to corral every scripture as though we are an expert. There is but one Shepard. There is but one High Priest. He presides over all His churches. We are not in charge. But we can offer ourselves as a living sacrifice for His benefit. He holds us all individually accountable, not collectively. If a self-prescribed Shepard presumes authority over a church, he endangers all within those walls even though he cannot save them. That kind of control is not an expression of freedom. The Spirit of God is the sole gatekeeper, not man. The Spirit of revival only comes to those who are free. Revival is the fruit of the Spirit of God.

Another appendage exists for consideration. There is also a self-professed Christian arm claiming no rights to the Holy Spirit. This faction interprets certain verses explaining the holy fire as bad by linking various negative-sounding verses. Their religion rejects the Holy Spirit of God by advocating that the Holy Fire is evil. While it would be quite easy to prove the Antichrist, the anti-religion, and Satan will be cast into the lake of fire, it would be more of a contextual cartwheel to propose that the fire at Pentecost is somehow also evil. This revision invites the rejection of the Holy Spirit.

Of course, rejection of the Holy Spirit is the single unforgivable sin. This underscores the regrouping around the core concept of the cross. Tacking on other criteria for membership should be seriously reconsidered. This acknowledgment alone should be enough to bring truth seekers to the point of reconciliation across man-made denominational lines.

At the first death, everyone must pass through the fire. Only those receiving the fire baptism will pass through the firewall unharmed into life everlasting. Everything un-pure will burn like chaff, Psalm 1. Rejecting the Holy Spirit excludes our only protection to eternal paradise. Blasphemy against the Holy Spirit negates our self-interest by trapping ourselves inside the fire of torment, unable to pass through. This cutting-off is referred to as a lake, rather than a river or spring of flowing water. God has informed all who will listen about this protection and how to access the Kingdom of Peace. To enter we must go through a purification process preceded in the belief of Yeshua's resurrection. Pentecost is the New Testament proof of everlasting power and existence. Here, we are left with the practical conception of fighting Pentecostal fire with consuming fire. Opting out only leads to hard times ahead. Those hardships will be faced alone, leading back to a lake with no escape. God is no respecter of persons. So, everyone is faced with this same dilemma. The choice is ours to make. Every tongue will confess that we all knew this Truth beforehand the foundations of the world. The disobedient will have only themselves to blame. As for believers who lived their faith, there is one additional caveat. They must forgive everyone, including non-believers. Otherwise, they attempt to hold a sovereign God accountable.

Yet, there is another group beyond the body. This cluster professes to be spiritual but not religious. They have a form of godliness with no lasting substance. Their arguments of faith resemble circular reasoning, and their philosophy revives two-thousand-year-old Zoroastrianism, otherwise known as environmentalism. Even though some in this group may have good intentions, such as exhibiting good stewardship of the earth's resources, it is not their central focus. Ultimately, the cause of our existence should be to extend the Gospel via imperfect beings, thereby glorifying God. If somehow, we think that we can Glorify God by omitting the testimony of Jesus Christ, which is to say denying the Holy Spirit, we deceive ourselves. As discussed, some people inherently live in self-deception. So, let's restate the issue and be clear; do not think for a moment that we can pass through the fire without the Holy Spirit. No one can be purified without fire, and we cannot become like Him unless the Holy Spirit is within us. This pathway leads to marriage with the Lamb and finally joining with Yahweh. In this way, the faithful are linked to the 3. Then, we can rejoin paradise anew. Again, this protection from the fire is only made available through the acceptance of the Messiah. There is no other access. Any claims to the contrary are merely man-made conjectures. Our hope rests in the resurrection power of Christ. His ascension is the only eyewitness account confirming resurrection in all of history. God holds the power of life and death. Many have set out to refute this resurrection on record. But every serious attempt to disprove accounts has been met with hard evidence to the contrary. Even still, most scoffers deny any genuine attempts to consider verifiable records. Most are too lazy to care or too scared to investigate appropriately. But this is ground zero. This is where the rubber meets the road. Jesus either rose from the dead or He did not. If He did not rise, he is merely a man. Likewise, the power of the Holy Spirit exists, or it does not. If we honestly observe those around us His invisible power can be seen changing lives for the better. His movement is like the wind, all around us. Yet, the irony is that only those who accept the Truth can experience it. How can a thirsty man who does not drink from a spring be quenched? Denying he is thirsty only starves the body. He will die thirsty though he claims otherwise. Moreover, he will remain thirsty into the next realm forever. Those with ears, let them here.

If we have come this far, our conscious man must conclude that the heart of man is deceitful. This awareness must admit that we are capable of self-preservation even to the point of masking illogical explanations as though they actually make sense. So, by man's own hands, he creates a mental dividing line whether inside or outside the body of Christ. Even the interpretations of holy scripture are not left unscathed. We must break away from any idea that we are a "good" person and die to the will of God to become His instrument for good. But, if we are susceptible to deceit at every turn, how can we know which way to turn? First, we must draw the line when the Spirit of God enters one's life. Or it does not. Then we proceed to turn over our control for God's purpose. For many, the essence of Leviathan resurfaces by fighting, "Who is in control?"

Here is the circle. We only live one life. Everyone must serve a master of their choosing. Furthermore, these are the last days and the final test for the church. Everyone must become more introspective if only to survive the hard times ahead. It should be no secret that self-analysis will be in short supply as the hourglass grains dissipate. People will be lovers of themselves. This will be apparent on many levels. Leaders will continue to profess the need for individuals to fellowship yet overlook that God professes the need for the whole church to unite in prayer. Perhaps all should take a page out of the example set forth by Kairos Prison Ministry. Kairos might be the best practical model for demonstrating how the church body should perform as one. All faiths should band together, united under the Good News of the Gospel putting aside differences. This is not a request to lay down one's individual beliefs. As the idea of a body suggests, there will always be as many interpretations of scripture as there are people. These differences are documented and necessary under the circumstances. This is a period of a divine call to observe the commandment of prayer and unity. If heeded, the resulting benefits would be millions uniting in the Spirit of the Lord. This bodily unification would dwarf the scriptural declaration that any two joined together are as ten thousand.

Some have professed the need to return to the book of Acts, which is to admit, among other things, a yearning for the Glory of God to return amongst men. Yet, this is unlikely on a large scale given the current conditions expressed moments ago. It is easier to surmise those days will not return inside most churches or with any significance simply because many espouse all the deeds within Acts died out with the Apostles. Surely, pockets of revival will continue to pop up as saving grace still exists. Any grandiose notion of a national revival lacks a crucial laissez-faire approach needed by Christian leadership. Internal church controls are far too embedded within today's culture to allow most pastors any spontaneousness. For example, multiple testimonies or other speakers are far and few between. This lack of insight and excessive structure places preconceived conditions upon the Spirit of God. Typically, the Spirit responds selectively under these conditions, sparsely choosing whosoever He wills. For this reason, God erroneously receives additional blame for His moderation. Instead, we should be more introspective and prayerful in thanks that He moves at all under these extreme conditions. Naturally, humanity and the powers of darkness are to blame for all the world's shortcomings. But blame is always easier to give than to receive.

So, we see how things get worse. Humanity's condition systematically ignores its' contributing shortcomings, beliefs, and control issues. In addition, mankind cultivates many of these errors only to present them as gospel truths. How emblematic it remains that the church is a weakened shadow of former glory as it displays a void of introspective inquiry into its' own inerrancies. Those searching for a resurgence of Acts should ask, "Are we granting free movement of the Spirit? Is the current course of the church maximizing growth and transformation? Are we living life more abundantly, or merely existing? Is the Spirit of God growing inside us as John 17 indicates?" Despite a quick verbal denial, our actions largely answer no to each question. Still, it is easier to deny all such things including apostles, power, and prophesy than to admit stifling God's free worship in Spirit and Truth. What will our decision be going forward? How much time remains? Will our end come before the Messiah returns?

There are several important statements to mention before closing this chapter, some of which we have briefly mentioned. Notice John 17 says the Father's love is in Jesus and Jesus is in every believer via the Holy Spirit. Christ indicates the church should be unified with God's glory, through Christ, just as the Father is in Him and He is in the Father. Ultimately, this completion of glorified unity occurs at the marriage to Yeshua as described in Revelation. Because Yeshua has obeyed and loved throughout His mission, we will share His sanctification through the commitment of marital union. All believers may share this abundant life by experiencing God's love through the growing gift of the Spirit. This gift grows from the inside out. It manifests itself in the Spiritual world but blooms for all to witness in this physical universe. This spiritual gift is the testimony of the authenticity of Jesus and the love the Father has for His own.

Putting a bow on this thought, the truth of Jesus as the Messianic Messenger and Son of God proclaims to the world that the Word of God was placed inside Mary's womb. Here we see a continuous pattern linking the Spirit to Emmanuel which is the perfect reflection of the Father. Also, let us not diminish the smallest detail; Eve came from the (inside) rib of Adam. Likewise, the Spirit God breathes scripture as we know it expressed by the written Word of God, the Bible. So, the scripture only lives by everything that precedes from the lips of God, not the other way around. Receiving that life is our only salvation. Living in that Rhema Spirit is our only avenue to maturity and salvation via the Word is the only Way back home once purified by fire. Those without a dominating spiritual fire within typically lean to verification of truth strictly through scripture. Although the spirit and scripture never contradict one another, the spirit may lead a disciple beyond the written text to suit the situation. For example, Peter would have never known Christ as the Messiah unless God had directly informed him. Another example: a leader outlined how he was called to a particular church to become the pastor. He correctly identifies receiving a Rhema Word directly from God. Conversely, clergy might state there can be no new revelation from God. All events must line up with the scripture. Yet, his Rhema Word to start a specific church wasn't in the Bible. Alas, this contradiction never seems obvious to most leaders. Herein is a snapshot of one illustration of how revelation is prohibited throughout numerous congregations today. They err on the side of no wildfire rather than any fire. The spicket of Truth is overruled by the flesh's capacity to control. The key to overcoming self-inflicted snares is learning the meaning of worshipping in Spirit and Truth.

All individuals completely void of spiritual fire have no source for divine revelation or vision. They are stunted. They harbor pockets of pride, untouched for correction. Therefore, they cannot wholly commit to obeying the Truth because they have not committed all areas of themselves. Here lies the difference between belief and obedience. Even though some deniers may come to believe in the Kingdom of God, they will never totally acquiesce. Some will avoid the whole truth their entire life. On the other hand, followers are to exhibit the Good News of the Spiritual Kingdom by loving one another. They do this by praying and obeying through the power of the Holy Spirit. These actions witness the Truth on earth since those without the fire cannot see into God's Spiritual Kingdom in heaven. This does not imply that the dark side has no power; it does. The spirit of control is one such widespread exhibition of evil frequently from pulpits. Now imagine, Jesus preaching at age 13 today inside a local church or synagogue. Just giving a brief testimony to most congregations is rare. Preachers don't liberally give up their time in the pulpit. True freedom of worship permits the preachers to preach, the prophets to prophesy, the healers to heal and the body to testify. When freedom is absent the spirit of control condemns the body. Plainly stated, though our words may speak as though we grant God His rightful responsibility to dispense grace to the faithful and the unfaithful, our actions covertly covet the Word of God thereby limiting the Spirit. By acquiescing control, we stretch ourselves in understanding and open the windows of heaven to receive the blessings of God. Of course, stretching oneself may not come without conflict. However, neither does the absence of conflict guarantee harmony. Although, it might conceal the root of the problem.

One final observation that is sure to rile many fronts. In John 17 Jesus prays for all those given to Him by God. Notice that He makes a point distinguishing between those of this world and those which belong to the Father. Those who eventually accept the Holy Spirit will be His and those who resist belong to the world. Whenever that saving point of grace occurs, it indicates God's sovereign timing. This should bring a serious moment of pause and understanding. Remember the example of Saul. Paul previously persecuted Christians unto death yet later he became a disciple of Christ. For this reason, forgiveness and grace must also be extended to believers and unbelievers alike. Had retribution come upon Paul before conversion it would have nullified his many great works designed to benefit the Kingdom after his epiphany. On the other, God's providence and sovereignty can never be thwarted. Moreover, herein is a glimpse that every life mission was preordained by the Creator just as Christ was before the foundation of the world. In this way, we understand that he who believes is not condemned, even before the foundations of the world but has everlasting life.

All of us have a divine purpose. All are loved. Not one is insignificant. For the elect to succeed in this realm, we need assistance from the only one who has flawlessly completed the race. The distinguishing characteristic in chapter 17 is that only the Son of God exercised perfection while operating in the flesh. Emmanuel conducted a perfect mission while operating in an imperfect environment. In and of itself, this is an unequaled feat, a miracle. A miracle only God with us could complete. We know this because all the elect have the same option to avoid falling short via the power of God, yet we continually err. Bluntly stated, if we do not kill the flesh, in the end, it will kill us.

THE BEGINNING AND BEYOND

Before Genesis outlined the foundations of the world there existed perfection. Many refer to this as paradise, others may call it heaven. This was all that was until some chose to follow imperfection. Since there can only be one creator, those selecting a new direction were permitted to follow imperfection, the opposite of all that was. All that was left to follow was not the Truth. Neither was it the Way of wisdom.

At first, the opposites had access to both worlds. Their newly ordained leader set out to adopt as many changes and rules as he desired. Every decree, by definition, was different from the order in which they originated. Some rules had more subtle alterations than others. All regulations were indefinitely subject to change and all decisions were arbitrary. Whatever suited the new leaders' fancy on any particular day ruled the realm. Anyone found breaking his laws, no matter how small, was sentenced to infinite conviction. The ultimate penalty equated to a loss of all choices which meant being locked away from the presence of all peaceful uniformity. But this was not evident from the start as each rule breaker continued deceiving themselves into believing that dual citizenship remained their continuous outlet to freedom. This seemed like a foregone conclusion, so they had no worries to the contrary. After approximately four thousand years had elapsed, a moment of surprise locked them out permanently, revoking any possibility of returning to the original peaceful environment. That day everything changed. That day their dual citizenship expired.

Since the Way back to their origin was now blocked, all new world residents were cut off inside the newer realm. They would be forever run by a leader who became judge, jury, and executioner. This new realm lacked any sense of peace because they were, and forever will be, opposites. There could only be one avenue of lawfulness, one written code of righteousness, and one Way to harmony. Therefore, the new world order would become a combatant even unto themselves, corrupted forever. Eventually, it would become clear to all, inside and out, that a house divided cannot stand.

To this day, several questions continuously resurface. First, "Why must the new order be opposite by definition?" All cohesive civilizations have codes and laws that produce order. Consider the premise of two worlds operating within differentiating conceptual models. Each realm runs on a specific set of mathematical, scientific, or natural laws depending on your terminology preference. Consider that each realm or domain is run by computer code. Currently, we define this code as a binary mathematical model of choices. Reasonably, any future modifications to the original perfect program can only produce results susceptible to error. Since the first realm presented the only perfect code in existence, no other solution will suffice. Altering this code for whatever purpose becomes an act of futility. Nonetheless, a persistent search for a second perfect code continues. As time marches closer to destiny, mankind still believes they can save themselves from this paradigm.

Faced with this dilemma of corruption from adaptation and the inability to return to a peaceful state of rest, each citizen could only perform results that continually produce faulty programming. To coin a phrase, one might suggest this outcome as a type of "cyber sin." The old saying used to be "Garbage in – garbage out." Yet, the only option seemingly available was to continue on this newly chosen programming path since the citizenship door to the first realm remained indefinitely closed. This realization of a doomed alternative program infuriated the new order, especially its leader. They asked, "Why is any other alternative impossible? Why is our way wrong? Why don't we celebrate differences and allow individual choices? Whatever happened to live and let live? Whatever happened to tolerance?" But in truth, their newly implemented corrupt code infected their original perfect nature. This virus would no longer allow them to coexist or intermingle peaceably in both domains. Plainly stated, perfection cannot exist with those who are willingly rebellious. Willful rebellion causes chaos. There exists our choice. Either one must cling to the perfect or the imperfect. This requires allegiance to one realm or the other. Thus, allegiance is made voluntarily to one leader or the other. Likewise, it is a fallacy that neither exists. Even serving oneself results in a de facto selection. Absolving oneself from choosing either master renders a deceitful illusion of self-control. It is another trap disguised as if to control one's own destiny. Truthfully, in the end, we must all serve somebody. That is our fate. We are not designed to be in total control. Our capacity is quite limited in and of itself. For many within this latter world, it is easier to don lifetime blinders than to acknowledge the necessity for assistance.

Confronted with the realization of tricking themselves into believing they were in control, one-third lashed outwardly to all that was accessible before them. Because they resented being locked out of paradise they blamed the Creator for His harsh rules, though justified and transparent. The adversary continued hurling charges against the Creator by demanding inclusiveness and diversity. The accuser attacked the motives of the Author suggesting that He must change the rules and loosen requirements so that all the disadvantaged could pass through into paradise once again. The deceiver declared that all citizens deserve a second chance at redemption. After all, he spouted that if the Author believed in Mercy and Grace, He should prove it by reinstituting permanent dual citizenship access. This view made logical sense to those suffering. After all, humanity claims no one deserves to suffer, right? However, feelings do not necessarily constitute reason or rules. Their reasoning ability became flawed after being locked out as they were all blinded by the choice to withdraw. Thus, their self-interest created a revocation from reason, not the other way around. Despite these facts, they refused to agree with the justified ruling in the slightest measure. They vowed to fight till the bitter end and by all means at their disposal. Their fight with reason continues to this very day. Nevertheless, frequency and volume do not produce logic. It merely wears down the opponent into submission. A lion without teeth can only gum his opponent to death.

The good Architect could not accommodate a rebellious group while simultaneously maintaining a perfectly peaceful environment. So, they were expelled. The decision to excommunicate one-third was dictated by an ongoing fiduciary duty to protect the faithful relationships of the remaining two-thirds. Furthermore, the Architect could never deny His true nature of sovereignty which constitutes His code. Thus, the decision to keep the status quo in paradise was always a foregone conclusion. Notwithstanding, with the creation of a new order came a new caveat. The new realm meant a new battleground would emerge upon the accuser's turf; winner takes all. The new world order now had a home-field advantage. This seemed to imply a shift of rules and dominion. That, too, would eventually prove to be an invalid assumption.

So, what then is the good Architect's goal? To let the Truth play out. To prove that original law is still true even inside a lawless world. Accomplishing this within a corrupted realm meant the message needed to be simple, separate, and unique. Ultimately, the "Good News" fulfilled all such requirements. The only thing left was to field a team. The pilgrims elected to the traveling team would be volunteers prepared to carry the "Good News" banner into a hostile work environment. All the while, the home team waited wrought with anger. They schemed a quite novel approach to winning. They planned to win by preventing all pilgrims from returning home, trapping them in the arena permanently. This approach schemed to trap the most souls on the field at the end of the game. Ultimately, any soul trapped would prove a victory for the new order. Ensnared souls would lose dual citizenship and imprison themselves permanently within the corrupted domain. Undoubtedly, the easiest way to accomplish this task would be to convince the incoming team to accept the newer fallible rules. A second rulebook would surely confuse the visiting team enough to ensure home-field victory dooming all who succumb to the deceit offered by this domain. Any rules clouding the judgment of players would be up for grabs.

Unbeknownst to the home team, a subprogram offers protection for all visitors, past, present, and future. It provides a pathway home and repairs all incurred damages. This protection plan had already been implemented even before the foundations of this world. In fact, prior to coming every elect incurred an independent download coded with the providence of God. Those invoking that power will win the battle and return home. Thus, this computer subprogram is equivalent to fighting fire with fire. In this way, all are predestined yet have free will. This is not man's current infected perception of free will which invites self-deception by infringing upon grace. In other words, for the elect, God's divine power either offers a sovereign gift delivered by providence or it doesn't. Consequently, rejection of that gift could only precede the reward. Thus, our limited human perception and corrupted need to control insists upon conjuring up scenarios that insert a previously decided personal decision. Once faced with this realization, we can begin to understand and gain wisdom. God's providence presents a supernaturally designed expectation of outcomes. It represents a Spiritual Being mindfully in control of all that is and all that will ever be. Chance plays no role in this distinct bottom-line computation. Nonetheless, we have free will to serve Him, or not, protected by the omnipotent Creator. This is justified because only He provides all that is good and without Him there is chaos.

Witnessing this world around us by His Spirit we perceive a code in chaos. We attempt to make sense of it all, but that endeavor rarely culminates in any logical solution or consensus. Things go astray sprouting from every leaky orifice. Others struggle constantly to redefine what is right and wrong. Double standards abound and become daily highlights of hypocrisy. Though the world seemingly offers avenues of helpfulness, these winding roads all lead to utter confusion and ultimate destruction. By now, most can admit this world's final testimony will end badly. Others venture to propose that man can save himself. For those persisting in denial, the end will only be evident after the fact. To them, it will appear to arrive swiftly. The final hurrah will witness man's code destroy itself when a soulless synthetic cipher turns on humanity. Every endless attempt at subprograms, workarounds, and patches will not turn off the A̲ndroid I̲nquisition. Nothing will subvert the inevitable consequences induced by a self-important attitude exhibited by the drive to control every single worldwide outcome. Let it be known the world leader, realizing he has lost the battle to impose total imprisonment, will conduct his final betrayal of all creation. His final betrayal will produce total annihilation. Thankfully, there remains one avenue of escape.

First, let us agree that governments have proven not to be the answer. They seemingly cannot help but impose restrictions of free will which only inflict harm to each inhabitant. For every good work they profess to solve two or more problems manifest themselves invoking pictures of the "Little Dutch Boy" who placed his fingers in the dike. Most admit to seeing the dam cracking; however, political disagreements usually ensue around who is the problematic person causing those cracks; and who should be sticking their fingers in the holes. Worldly discussions propose an endless slew of push-and-pull solutions only producing more muddy waters. History demonstrates how governments attempt to coerce and control the masses. Sometimes control manifests itself through religious outlets. Some governments deny religious expression unless it falsely projects God. This is designed to prevent the intrusion of Sovereign power from usurping governmental control over individuals. It is a must-have part of the authoritarian program. This is because prayer supersedes earthly authority, even personal control. It cannot be understated that prayer is the most important tool to exercise over every adversity. To effectively petition this power of prayer it is helpful to grasp the insight that this fight exists on a spiritual level even though concrete adversaries are presented before us. These adversaries may work through an average individual, businesses, and governments. Specifically, only the fallen one-third are directly behind the confrontations plaguing humanity. Since they were once heavenly creatures, they still possess certain knowledge about God and heaven. These original beings likely observed the creation of the universe, and the declarations recorded in the book of Genesis, etcetera. They likely witnessed some or all of the recorded books in heaven spoken of in scripture. They have watched each century pass and the fulfillment of the ages just as the Word foretold. This equates to firsthand knowledge of all history up to this point in time. They likely have their own books of record. They can never forget their loss of dual citizenship which sealed their eternal fate at the seventh seal of silence as illuminated in Revelation Made EZ. Witnessing all these events unfold, the fallen one-third know time is short. They will most assuredly become more diligent, designing a multitude of disasters and snares for mankind until the last moment in time as we know it.

Since the creation of time must play a meaningful clue along this winding road to destruction, exploring that process from Genesis to the present should give us some insight into the urgency of the current day. One might consider the first hurdle to address is the age of creation itself. Scientists have tools to ascertain the age of trees, fossils, etc., which suggest a contrarian viewpoint toward traditional Christianity. The proverbial question arises, "Which came first, the chicken or the egg?" While this question may appear debatable, there is likely only one simple answer.

Since Adam and Eve were formed out of the dust of the ground, they must have been fully created all at once. Therefore, we can logically ascertain that all of creation was fully matured. This would account for a mature tree containing carbon that otherwise would indicate centuries of existence, not to mention recent carbon dating discrepancies. From this perspective, the answer to the "chicken or the egg" comes to light.

Notwithstanding, attempting to date the age of Adam and Eve from this vantage point also appears futile and possibly insignificant to our quest. Therefore, a responsible course of action must be undertaken to tackle the passage of time, directly. Furthermore, if we responsibly pursue this avenue, it may give a clearer understanding of current events, whether imminent, catastrophic, or otherwise. Using this strategy exposes one action to be superior. Examining Genesis, scripture states that God created the universe in 6 days, and rested on the 7th. Most scholars believe mankind will have approximately 6000 years before the 7th-day millennial reign of Christ begins. Since each day represents 1000 years, 6 days equals 6,000 years. If this religious claim is true, certain information within the scripture must be supplied. Of course, this implies that all information is to be interpreted and applied correctly. As demonstrated throughout history this is a constant refining process. Personal experience has convinced me that supporting evidence exists though it must be revealed through revelation by the Holy Ghost. This is true for all scripture. Thus, all knowledge is truth. And, all truth is distributed by God. Since man's history is littered with vain attempts to control knowledge and outcomes, we must be careful not to maintain any hold of predetermined measures that would result in the same pitfalls of the past. Let us push on from here, with the goal of unity in mind continuing our search for knowledge starting with Genesis.

Centuries ago, a highly respected Archbishop of Ireland was greatly ridiculed for declaring that the first day of creation arrived at the autumn equinox. Sadly, this act of scorn is not uncommon even within the church. Though we cannot chase every wind of doctrine, prayer, and reasoning should abound as we seek unity, honor, and respect with our brothers in Christ. In that light, let us consider the reasoning of James Ussher, and some of his thoughts for that first creation year suggested as 4004 BC. His evaluation of chronological events may be sound enough to give a launching platform assisting us in our endeavor to define the present era. In the next diagram, we see a first glimpse of how Scripture uses events as a timetable. This construct was established from the beginning and will be the format repeatedly utilized by Daniel as well as Revelation. The reasoning for an event-based structure is paramount. Calendars will purposely be changed to hide the significance of future coming days. Therefore, great care is always necessary when converting one calendar period to the next. So, while the purpose of new calendar systems can be helpful to guide a more precise yearly system of measurement, they have also created obstructions to historical accuracy. Though legitimate, for the moment this is a sidebar issue which we will currently abstain from commenting in lieu of the bigger picture.

Here is how the process unfolds from the perspective of James Ussher beginning in 4004 BC:

Total Years	Event	Book	Date
130	2nd appointed - Seth born when 1st man - Adam was 130	Genesis 5:3	3874 BC
235	3rd mortal - Enos born when Seth was 105	Genesis 5:6	3769 BC

325	4th sorrow - Cainan born when Enos was 90	Genesis 5:9	3679 BC
395	5th blessed God - Mahalaleel born when Cainan was 70	Genesis 5:12	3609 BC
460	6th come down - Jared born when Mahalaleel was 65	Genesis 5:15	3544 BC
622	7th teacher - Enoc born when Jared was 162	Genesis 5:18	3382 BC
687	8th death brings - Methuselah born when Enoch was 65	Genesis 5:21	3317 BC
874	9th despairing - Lamech born when Methuselah was 187	Genesis 5:25	3130 BC
1056	10th rest - Noah born when Lamech was 182	Genesis 5:28	2948 BC
1558	Shem born when Noah was 502 (1556)	Genesis 11:10	2446 BC
1656	Flood arrived when Noah was 600	Genesis 7:6	2348 BC
1658	Arphaxad born when Shem was 100	Genesis 11:10	2346 BC

1693	Salah born when Arphaxad was 35	Genesis 11:12	2311 BC
1723	Eber born when Salah was 30	Genesis 11:14	2281 BC
1758	Peleg born when Eber was 34 (1757)	Genesis 11:16	2246 BC
1787	Reu born when Peleg was 30	Genesis 11:18	2217 BC
1819	Serug born when Reu was 32	Genesis 11:20	2185 BC
1849	Nahor born when Serug was 30 (1848)	Genesis 11:22	2155 BC
1878	Terah born when Nahor was 29	Genesis 11:24	2126 BC
2008	Abraham born when *Terah was 130	Genesis 11:32, 12:4	1996 BC
2083	Abraham enters Canaan at 75	Genesis 12:4	1921 BC
2513	Exodus of the Jews from Egypt (430 years of slavery)	Exodus 12:40	1491 BC
3420	Last deportation of the Jews	3420+584= 4004	584 BC

4000	Birth of Christ	Acts 12	*4-3 BC
6000 Years	=4000 Old Testament + 2000 N.T. Grace	Genesis-Revelation	1997

Several points of interest arise from this chronology. First, is the recognition of the remarkable precision of time and events unfolding just as presumed by ancient theologians for centuries. 6000 years are beginning to be revealed like a scroll unraveling before our eyes pointing precisely at the birth of Christ. On the other hand, the possibility of errors begins with the creation's starting date continuing beyond the interpretation of certain scriptures, such as Abraham's highly contested date of birth. Many, including me, have assumed that because Genesis states Terah lived 70 years and begot Abram, Nahor, and Haran, it was definitive proof Abraham was born 1948 years from Adam. However, Abraham was the third born some 60 years later. This is clarified by Abraham's departure from Haran which occurred after his father's death at age 75 when Terah was 205. Thus, Abraham is listed first because of his Messianic lineage just as Shem is listed as a firstborn yet was likely born 2 years later. Third, even in lineage, it is important to remember that numbers have meaning. In both (2) cases, the 1st (of 3) shall be last; 3 is also symbolic for Christ.

Next, some will give umbrage to the Exodus period charted. There are various disagreements concerning several circumstances and possibilities surrounding the exact date. For now, let us assume the scripture has directed us at least approximately to the period of Herod the Great. Thusly, perhaps we can at least partially substantiate the Exodus date by searching for confirmation of any other scripture interacting with the birth of Christ. Our primary focus is to find any anchor points leading forward an additional 2000 years illuminating meaningful material to our present-day circumstances. Some anchor dates are exhibited in several different charts distributed in assorted chapters. All the charts are plausible. One or some of those charts as a collection are likely correct. This truth will bear out by the end of this book.

Finally, just as the names of the twelve tribes of Israel spell a wonderful message as revealed elsewhere in the book series, so do the names of the first 10 generations from Adam to Noah. Both model a generational promise to fulfill the covenant of restoration:

> Man was appointed mortal sorrow, but the blessed God will come down as a teacher; death brings a despairing rest.

This promise has been delivered. We know this as the "Good News" of Christ. It was first offered to the Jews and then to the Greeks. Now, later the last becomes the first…

AGE TO AGE

A few years ago, I saw a Movie about an atheist who set out to disprove the existence of God. The main character figured disproving that the resurrection of Christ had ever occurred would tumble the main pillar of Christian dogma. This remains a perfectly logical perspective since Christianity retains its unique position as the only religion to exhibit eyewitness resurrection testimony. Several books have been written using this perspective and Lee Strobel's movie would be produced as a direct result of one of these written attempts. What Lee did not surmise prior to his quest was his impending conversion. Lee spent two years in his pursuit before concluding that it would take more faith to maintain atheism than to accept the facts unfolding before him. Lee eventually embraced the idea of a risen Messiah and became a disciple. You might say Lee was a modern-day "doubting Thomas."

Perhaps this story fascinated me because a similar disbelief resides within the church congregations today or maybe I see parts of myself in Lee. Analytical minds think in specific patterns that all tend to lead to the same conclusions. I, too, began a similar parallel path in search of answers. Although, my route seeks details about a taboo destination. So, unlike the movie, this next chapter does not seek to prove the resurrection specifically. Rather, the following chapter builds upon a cycle of recorded events and clues within the 6,000 years previously established. This is partly accomplished by including the birth of Jesus. Furthermore, this book does not firmly debate the possibility of millions or thousands of earth years before man's creation. One can only speculate how long a God Day of creation equates to Earth years. Though some may apply scripture loosely suggesting a day is as a thousand years; but, before Adam, we cannot be sure of the number of applicable hours in a day. Therefore, the appropriate elapsed time could be far greater than anticipated, or even far less depending on one's perspective. In Ussher's example, earth time begins around day 4 of 7, 4004 B.C. His research suggests all 7 days remain a constant 24-hour period just as we recognize them today. Regardless, our enlightenment may not be dependent on these far-reaching unknowns. Therefore, let us press forward, if only temporarily toward an in-depth search for insight from multiple venues.

As documented by James Ussher, our current course of events has led us to approximate 4-3 B.C. as the birth of Christ. But is this an accurate date? Scholars and writers, such as Murrell Selden and Craig Chester, have spent countless hours studying King Herod's death and historian Josephus' writings. Their painstaking research reflects many moving parts such as wars, constellations, astrology, scriptures, historical documentation, government changes, actions, etcetera. The first important pivot was the death of Herod the Great likely occurring in 1 B.C., several years after being stricken ill and abdicating his throne. This debated date more appropriately permits certain events alluded to above including Herod's order to kill all male infants under the age of 2. In addition, if Jesus were born around the autumn equinox of 3 B.C. it would closely align with Ussher's view of creation.

    1 B.C. Herod's death
    -2-year decree
    3 B.C. Christ birth

Ernest Martin also supports Christ's birthdate as 3 BC. Ernest points out that John 4:35 is the link indicating that Jesus's ministry began in a Sabbatical year. Autumn 27 A.D.

through 28 A.D. can be identified as a Sabbatical year. Since Jesus was about 30 years of age at this time, His birth could be deduced as 3 B.C. with relative certainty. The significance of a Sabbatical year has other implications as well. During the Sabbatical, there was no sowing and reaping so people had more free time than during harvesting years. Since Jews were required to visit the Holy City of Jerusalem for different feasts, no harvesting duties permitted more flexibility for travel. This revelation clarifies why so many people were available to hear the Good News preached by Jesus as well as John the Baptist. In short, Martin eventually concludes that Jesus must have been born on the autumn equinox of 9/11, 3 B.C., possibly at 7 pm. However, any hour after dusk would have been viewed as the next day on a Jewish calendar. So, if Jesus' birth occurred at 7 pm it would have been the previous night by today's standards. In any event, the fall equinox typically occurs around the 3rd week of September. In 3 B.C., Jerusalem's equinox fell on Friday 9/22 at 3:43 pm. Other locations register the account on Saturday 9/23. More significantly, the Feast of Trumpets fell on Martin's 9/11 hypothesis. As we examine this festival in later chapters this appears to be prophetically substantiated. There are also valid arguments that endorse December 25th as accurate. Regardless, the year certainly aligns. The 9/11 date is also highly recognizable in recent U.S. history as well. The Twin Tower disaster in New York City could be portrayed as an act of terrorism perpetrated on a Christian nation, albeit a nation in rebellion.

To recap, thus far James Usher has led us to transverse 4 thousand years to the birth of Christ, a new era introducing the "Good News" gospel of grace. If we agree with Augustine of Hippo, there are 6/7 Ages of the World from Adam through Revelation. This is consistent with most Jewish theology as well. Others choose to divide the Ages into 3-4 categories. Under these conditions, if each age lasts approximately 1,000 years it places us at, or near the end of the 6th age. The following calculations place 6,000 years ending in 1997 A.D.

1,000	Years per age
x 6	Ages
6,000	Total time

4004 BC	Ussher's creation
-6,000	Skip year zero
1997 AD	Last age precipice

If Augustine of Hippo is correct, this places our current year at the precipice of the 7th Age. For the church, a 7th age is thought to incorporate a millennial reign and may even run parallel to the 6 Ages of this world as inferred in the book series (Revelation Made EZ & Seer in the Way). Below we can see the representation of the 7 days of creation lasting 7,000 years, each day for a thousand years until the 7th day of rest. Today the 7th day of rest is still acknowledged as the Sabbath in many religious circles which we identify as Saturday. Lost in this context is the perfect connection to a 1,000-year millennial reign. As we will explore later, every 7th year is called the Shmita year, or Sabbath of the Land. Nothing was to be harvested, and the land was to be left untilled. God's parallel between the day of rest and the millennial reign becomes evident.

Our query must squarely examine if this 7th day of fallow is presently underway, and the preparation of a new 1,000-year peaceful reign is upon us. Do our current worldwide circumstances warrant such an inquiry? The news reports state impending World War III events as imminent. An honest assessment of our surroundings shows constant conflict and ginning up of worldwide circumstances. The best description of this world illustrates impatience, propaganda, unkindness, incompetency, and chaos. All these antagonistic qualities were accelerated in the name of tolerance and diversity. These values have promoted a society of self-absorbed citizens. Moreover, society has demanded these values. This unsound behavior has brought us to this point of no return. Make no mistake, attitude, directly and indirectly, affects future events' circumstances. From here the leap leading to a feelings-based society drives a culture into a proverbial ditch. Any society acting solely upon feelings becomes irrational, unpredictable, and unstable. Full circle, all decision-based behaviors or feelings produce consequences. Contrary to popular psychology, all justification founded on feelings leaves little or no common ground for a solution-based society. People simply no longer decide to listen to reason. Just as in the days of Noah. Therefore, we can reasonably surmise that the 7th Age is likely upon us.

Having established the 7 Ages, we can approximate Jesus having been born toward the end of the 4th Age of 7. The 5th Age of Grace begins sometime after His birth; more specifically this may refer to the period after Yeshua's resurrection such as the 50th day of Pentecost. The 1st Trumpet of Christ's Kingship likely announces this new dominion era. The 7th seal of silence followed by the 1st New Testament Trumpet was referenced in greater detail in the second book of the series, Seer in the Way. Below are estimates of all 7 Ages:

Total Years	Event	Book	Date
130	Adam-Noah	Age 1 1000 yrs.+	4004 BC 2948 BC
1056	Noah was 600 yrs. old when the flood arrived.	Age 2 1056-1656	2948 BC 1921 BC
2083	Abraham called & entered Cannan at 75- Saul, David, Solomon	Age 3 Covenant	1921 BC 930 BC

3074	Saul, David, Solomon-Messiah	Age 4 O.T. Kingdom	930 BC 4-30 AD
4004	Messiah-Schism 7th Seal/1st Trumpet	Age 5 N.T. Kingdom	4-30 AD 1054 AD
5058	Schism & Super Nova 4004-6000=1997 AD	Age 6 New Israel	1054 AD 1997 AD
6000	Present day - Awaiting 7th Trumpet	Age 6-7	1997 AD- 2047 AD
6041	Present-Rapture		Quest
6051	Rapture-Armageddon		Quest
	New Jerusalem	Age 7	Eternity

Of course, others have added different interpretations of the Ages after Augustine. Some might conclude the best summation of Augustine's Ages divides them into three sub-components. The fourth denotes a return to the original condition of creation harmony. Numerically, 3 represents Christ; 4 is the distance between heaven and Earth or the appointed times, directly referencing God's Holy Festivals.

Chaos	Adam-Abraham	Age 1	4004 - 2004 BC

Law	Abraham-Christ	Age 2	2004 - 3 BC
Grace	Christ-6,000 years	Age 3	3 BC - 1997 AD
Paradise	Millenium / New Jerusalem	Age 4	1997 AD - Eternity

Now that we have a loose understanding of where we have been and where we intend to go, Genesis 6 presents itself. Genesis 6 is widely thought to express either the time elapsed until the flood or the eventual maximum lifespan of humans... 120 years. But what if this context had additional meaning? What if the days of Noah were mirrored within this specific statement? What would that look like?

Our current theme rests on the premise that mankind began around 4004 B.C. and expects to arrive at a final destination approximately in 6,000 years laboring through the 4-7 Ages. Applying Genesis 6 to the Ages might also link Genesis 1, creation, and generations. For example, suppose 120 years was not just a signal of when flood waters would arrive but also a timeline of generations until the end of days. In that case, 120 years could be a cyclical period of Godly events or have generational implications; this is not meant to cast confusion upon the type of generations spoken of by Moses in Psalms 90, which references the life span of an average human to 70-80 years. So, let us explore some possibilities that may apply more understanding when calculating 120.

120 generations through 4-7 Ages:

>6000 years
>/120 generations
>= 50 cycles/events

A simple division of 6000 years by 120 generations equates to 50 cycles. But the result leaves a question in and of itself. What does 50 represent and is it significant? Is the number 120 of any importance? As discussed earlier, 120 denotes a divinely appointed time of waiting for repentance specifically before the arrival of flood waters. In addition, 120 marked the waiting age of several prominent figures who were granted birth of a child. 3 kings ruled Israel for 120 years; Saul, David, and Solomon ruled from 1050 to 930 B.C. 120 marked the age Moses passed away and echoed his penance by the lack of his entry into the Holy Land. Moses' life was divided into 3 stages of 40 years (to be examined with the number 40). More pertinent to this quest remain the following two examples:

1. In the Old Testament, 120 priests accompanied King Solomon when the Ark of the Covenant was brought to Jerusalem.

2. In the New Testament, 120 disciples were present during the Ascension of Christ. Since Christ symbolizes a new Ark within each believer spiritually, does this confirm He will return sometime after 6000 years for His disciples?

   4004 BC approximate beginning
   -6000 years = 120 generations x 50 cycles
   = 1997 AD

Likewise, the number 50 does not appear to be arbitrary. In the Old Testament, 50 represents a special time for remission of sins and debt forgiveness. A special Jubilee celebration was marked to occur every 50th year at the end of a Sabbatical Cycle. Throughout this time of Jubilee, all persons and lands were required to rest just as described during a normal Saturday Sabbath. The word Jubilee means deliverance. In the New Testament, the word Pentecost means 50th as it marks the arrival of a Spiritual Kingdom 50 days after the resurrection of the Messiah's crucifixion. For some reason, it is not widely known among Christian congregations that Yeshua's ascension did not occur until 40 days after His resurrection. 10 days following that live ascension was declared as Pentecost. Pentecost marks the delivery of the Spiritual Kingdom of God inside each individual referred to as a bodily tabernacle. Could these be two of the missing components that Jews and Christians have overlooked? Is it possible that the anticipated temple has already been constructed within every believer? Are religious people looking for a Kingdom that has already arrived? As this calculation supports delivery into the 7th Age, it warrants asking if the word Jubilee is trying to tell us that something monumental is about to transpire. Is the 7th Age showing us an era of rest for the whole Earth is upon us? Does this era arrive on a Jubilee year? Does this imply that a 1000-year Sabbath rest occurs void of all mankind, after a World War III event? Is this final 7th Age a Pentecostal-type transition from flesh entirely to Spirit? Or will some people survive?

Still, there is yet another mention of generations in scripture which may help answer when this last 7th era might befall us. Within the book of Matthew appears the genealogy of Jesus Christ. Revealed are 3 sets of 14 generations. The 1st set begins with Abraham through King David. The 2nd set continues with David till Josiah or the Babylonian exile. The 3rd set continues with exile through Joseph and Mary to Jesus. The dilemma from here is determining if there is a 4th set of 14 generations from the birth of Christ forward. What empire(s), person(s), or time frame might represent 14 generations? To my knowledge, there is no blanket discovery for any specified length of time for 14 generations. Both previous books have revealed these discoveries by mapping time through empires. However, there may be an interesting discovery extending from the dates of Adam through Abraham. When using Ussher's chart, the next calculation produces interesting results:

```
4004 B.C.    Adam
-1996 B.C.   Abraham
= 1996/7     A.D. +1 Mirror
```

Over the past few years, I have noticed that several phenomena periodically reoccur. Select dates from the Old Testament reflect timelines in the New Testament. Many of those circumstances have a valid basis for justification. In this case, both dates used are highly speculative and should not be considered sole supporting documentation. On the other hand, it may help bolster the case, provided more research leads to similar conclusions. This calculation implies a new beginning with Abraham and again at the end of the 7th Age in 1997.

Finally, it is worth mentioning that the number 14, like Jubilee, represents deliverance or salvation. Breaking down 14 equates to 2 x 7; 7 signifies perfection, the Word, creation, and completeness; 2 is associated with incarnation, denoting the possibility of Father, Son deity. 2 and 7 combined portray a clearer image of Emmanuel, God with us in perfection. Since the genealogy period was discontinued at the Messiah's birth, it further demonstrates completion as confirmed by John 19:30. It is worth mentioning that unfortunately, much of the genealogical documentation and Jubilee records were lost in Babylonian captivity. Otherwise, our quest would prove elementary. Still, we have placed the year of Yeshua's birth, and conceivably the birth of Israel marks the final piece of the generational puzzle. These events will act as a springboard propelling our quest forward.

LET THE FEAST BEGIN

My first up-close experience with Passover was in my earlier years, around 13. Some apartment neighbors invited me to join them for dinner. Jarette was my first Jewish friend outside of sports. Before that, I had a few baseball, and football teammates who were Jewish, and one coach whom I played for several years in both sports. The Jewish community always seemed set apart, but I consistently extended my hand in loving friendship even during these early years. For me, there was a kinship that I could not pinpoint. The camaraderie exemplified within their culture uniquely warmed me. Anyway, Jarette found it difficult to fit in with other kids our age. So, I made a special effort to be his buddy. His parents were great people, and I found them kind and intelligent. They introduced me to the nuances of an authentic Passover meal. The supper was regimented, yet warm and inviting. As the meal progressed, it became obvious that each dish had a particular order of consumption. Before serving a course, the head of the table announced the symbolism of each food. It was quite a lengthy process, but I didn't mind. It was all new to me, yet deep down, I felt we all shared the same theme. That dinner experience stuck with me my entire life.

During the year or two we all shared, they loved to call me Jeremiah, after the original Old Testament version of my given name. They seemed to treat me more like one of their own than an outsider. It made me feel special and loved.

Once they verbalized their belief that I must be of Jewish descent. That belief must have been based on more than the fact that we all shared blue eyes, although Jarette had one mixed green and blue color in his left eye. Nonetheless, somewhere deep inside I believed that to be a true statement but, at the time, I couldn't prove it or know why I felt that way. I just did. Regardless, we all got along quite well. They were patient with me and forgiving of our differences. They never forced me to eat or do anything I did not want to, like wear the small Jewish hats men don, although I would have if they had asked. For all these reasons and others, I enjoyed visiting whenever invited. But after about 2 years they moved away, and we lost contact. As months turned into years, I became increasingly disappointed that we had not spent more time together. Perhaps that is merely a matter of perspective, and I should be more grateful for the time we shared rather than the time we could have. On the other hand, my view could be clouded by various future visiting instances that did not produce that desired effect. Anyway, moments like this make me reflect on lovely people in my past who shared special occasions along the way. It can be said that we are all composites of our past experiences. And, now, God has led me full circle to discuss this Passover Feast.

In the previous chapter, we determined the number 4 directly reflected God's High Holy Feasts. Each feast is an event acknowledging God's appointed times. Several events have been fulfilled and some are yet to come. Since His festival plans are a preordained sequence of events, they should be recognizable for every nation and peoples throughout all the Ages. Leviticus 23 outlines Israelite festivals and gives instructions for observing the practice. Accompanying these events are stories that symbolically depict God's plan of redemption and deliverance transitioning into eternity. Each event portrays a piece of the puzzle across the Ages until time inevitably concludes.

Therefore, exploring each festival individually and collectively is mandatory when determining the relevance to end-time dates.

The first festival to examine is perhaps the most known Jewish holiday called Passover which most Christians associate with Easter. Although they are not actually the same holiday, they partially overlap in springtime as does the Festival of Unleavened Bread and Firstfruits. Passover commemorates the Jewish exodus from 400 years of Egyptian bondage. The feast received its' name as the angel of death passed over every home with lamb's blood smeared over the threshold sparing their first-born male child within. This was the 10th plague Moses decreed to Pharoah in the Old Testament. Easter celebrates the New Testament resurrection of the Messiah. All these occasions honor the same Father and point to salvation, though Easter recognizes redemptive hope through Christ.

The first Passover occurred at Mount Sinai as recorded in Numbers 9 (after departing Egypt's plagues). Thus, Jews would say the Old Testament God alone redeemed Israel, dismissing the New Testament Messiah as having already arrived. Other names for Passover are Pesach, Springtime Festival, Feast of Unleavened Bread, and Matzo, with several other Hebrew translations and variations. Notwithstanding, Passover and the Feast of Unleavened Bread were originally separate festivals. Today they are celebrated as one 7-day event. Delving into the modifications between these next two events will disclose additional keys differentiating Judaism and Christianity. With divine guidance, these differences may help us to conclude when the last days shall commence. In this light, we will seek all relevant information God decides to disclose. For, without His disclosure, our search is in vain. Suffer a while longer and see what is in store.

Basic knowledge of the Lord's Passover tells us it was a designated time to bring the Paschal lamb sacrifices to the Temple in Jerusalem. An unblemished 1-year-old male lamb was selected on the 10th day of Nissan and held 4 days until its' slaughter on the 14th. Pesach, or Passover, was ordered to be celebrated each spring at dusk on the 14th day of the first month of Nissan, sometimes called Aviv. Two important clarifications need to be addressed that have produced confusion. First, dusk, or evening, would be considered "the beginning" of each day just as Springtime shares the same interpretation. Second, since the Passover and Unleavened Bread festivals have been combined the start date was moved to the 15th of Nissan. Nissan is a Babylonian word more commonly used today, while Aviv is the Hebrew equivalent. Sacrifices were conducted on the full moon in this first month. In fact, all events revolve around a 30-day lunar calendar cycle, 12 months, 360 days a year. Of course, today our calendar has 365 days. This is one reason scripture explicitly instructs us to take notice of seasonal signs, Ecclesiastes 3 and Matthew 24, rather than historical alterations of the calendar. Every year the seasons seem to come and go with little regard by most, with the exception of farmers, even though seasons are essential to our way of life. Spring, summer, winter, and fall are divinely designed to endure throughout the ages. In this way, feasts are intertwined with scriptural feasts as an unbreakable timetable. Accordingly, all four seasons have symbolic associations. For example, just as nature is reborn in springtime, the Exodus and the first resurrection ensue after the barley harvest in springtime. In this analogy, Passover becomes a symbolic reminder of rebirth or deliverance from all animalistic passions of living (to the eventual divinely controlled aspects of Spirituality found after Shavuot as depicted by wheat offerings). Jews may relate this redemptive act to Noah's flood while Christians point directly to Calvary's cross. Nonetheless, many places in the

Old and New Testament produce satisfactory references in this light. For our purposes, this context of deliverance can not only be seen as a one-time sacrificial lamb but also as corresponding to the eventual return of Yeshua, Revelation 11. English translates the Hebrew word Yeshua as Jesus, meaning God saves. Some Christians associate Yeshua's return at the 7th trumpet with the phrase "caught up" as found in 1 Thessalonians, 4. Many have coined the word "rapture" to articulate this idea though the word is not specifically found in scripture. Most of the rapture debate revolves around when Christ returns, not if he returns. In other words, will Yeshua return before a final battle, after Armageddon, or both?

Revisiting the previous chart, we can reasonably add the final sounding of an expected 7th trumpet is likely to coincide with the 7th Age. And, if this imminent 7th trumpet is the day of harvest, there are viable questions to consider. First, will Jesus return at some point during this special spring festival? Will Jesus' return occur on the 10th day of Nissan? Or will Yeshua's return occur on the 14th? Why hasn't Christ already come back? Perhaps the 14th refers to 14 generations.

4004	Messiah-7th Seal	Age 5	30 A.D.
5058	Messiah-Schism	Age 6	1054 AD
6000	Schism-7th Trumpet	Age 7	1997 AD
6041	Present-Rapture	Age 7	
6051	Rapture-Armageddon	Age 7	

| 6051 | Millenium/New Jerusalem | Age 7 | Eternity |

Examining some of the previous numbers knits together some reoccurring themes that should be addressed before proceeding. Again, Passover is supposed to be supper on the evening of the 14th called a Seder. According to the Torah, Unleavened Bread begins the following night, lasting 7 days from the 15th through the 21st. Interestingly, those outside Jerusalem may extend the 7-day portion of the festival until the 8th day. So, technically, the modern-day festival already lasts 8 days with the possibility of a 9th. A Jubilee celebration also occurs in the 8th year of a Sabbatical year. Some believe a Jubilee can extend into another year as well. Could it be possible that those outside of Jerusalem needing that extra year for conformity symbolize New Testament Christians? As we will reference repeatedly, Noah was also considered the 8th person on the ark. Could Noah's story be another reflection of the gentile's salvation through the living water, John 4:10-14?

Next, the Paschal lamb was to be prepared with no broken bones, John 19. It was to be eaten with bitter herbs as a reminder of Egyptian bondage. These spring feasts mimic the Day of Atonement. The highest holy Day of Atonement also begins on the 10th day of the 7th month. Both dates are a picture of sin removal depicting Christ as our Passover blood atonement, 1 Corinthians 5. They seem to demand a self-assessment as though each one of us has been individually liberated from implied Egyptian bondage. In Revelation, the number 10 expresses God's power in depicting punishment under the law. In summation, 10 symbolizes God's law and power as shown in the 10 commandments and Genesis 1 when "God's said" 10 times. Moses is said to have rested 10 days before returning up Mount Sinai after angrily breaking the first set of tablets. God produces 2 replacement stones with 5 commandments on each. In the Old Testament 3000 die as a result of lawful disobedience and in the New Testament 3000 are saved by the Good News of Calvary's Cross. These circumstances draw a mirror image between God the Father and God the Son.

Third, as discussed, Yeshua is the 3rd set of 14 generations ending with Joseph and Mary. Here we see that the 14th day implies a double measure of spiritual perfection, the second Godhead who delivers atonement. Though most believers are of the opinion that the 2nd coming of Christ is a rapture event, scripture indicates Jesus will return yet again to complete another cycle on Earth at Armageddon (or before). This confirmation is evident as Revelation clearly describes the High Priest wearing white garments inside the Temple of Jerusalem holding bowls full of sacrifices from the saints. This ritual culminates in the destruction of all remaining earthly adversaries. Most interestingly, there are also 14 years between Ishmael and Isaac. Could the number 14 signify the period passing over the first male birthright of Ishmael to Isaac? Is this a clue signaling that a rapture may occur 14 years before New Jerusalem arrives? Or does 14 correspond to the Exodus and Jubilee year going forward?

Principally, Passover and Unleavened Bread bear witness to the resurrection of Yeshua for all believers. In the current charts, if Jesus died in 30 A.D. and the temple was destroyed in 70 A.D., this would account for a 40-year gap when the feast no longer was conducted inside temple walls. In other words, since Jesus already met His fate on the cross, there was no future implication for a repetitive lamb sacrifice. All sins were forever forgiven for those who believed. This is verified in Revelation as a New "sinless" Jerusalem will be restored and reserved only for believers. Again, it should not go unnoticed that historically virtually all sacrifices stopped after the destruction of the holy temple in 70 A.D. Sometime beforehand the Passover feast retreated inside home observances. Could it be that the eyewitness accounts of the ascension were an integral factor of this phenomenon? Luke 22 addresses the 7 days of Unleavened Bread as sinless. In Hebrew 4, Christians suggest the visual exterior of matzah (flatbread) represents the piercing and stripes of Christ as found in Isaiah 53 and 1 Peter 2. The Gospel of John emphasizes Jesus as the bread of life in chapter 6. Therefore, it would be a dereliction of duty to overlook that Jesus' last week prior to the crucifixion was cut in half (only to rise from the dead 3 days and nights later) as documented by varied eyewitnesses, 1 Corinthians 15. Sadly, eyewitness accounts mean little to doubters unless in a court of law. But this crucifixion week should demand notice as the whole idea corresponds specifically to the Festival of Unleavened Bread. This celebration is considered the 1st of 3 major festivals. Thus, Unleavened Bread is the introduction of events, not the conclusion. Some scriptures mention a total of 4 major feasts, but the 4th may be a heavenly banquet on behalf of the saint's marriage to the Lamb in Revelation 19. Or could it be possible that the 4th feast in question also occurs on the 14th? Will the selection of a bride be made on the 10th? Could these celebration days translate into earthly years, drawing us a picture of a waiting period until the marriage to the lamb of God? If the first group of feasts depicts Yeshua's salvation, why wouldn't the final 4 feasts be equally important? These questions are not meant to sound premature. Rather, let us answer them moving forward in due time.

The 3rd Feast is Firstfruits, Feast of Your Harvest, or Counting of the Omer. Firstfruits is often considered a continuation of Passover and sometimes conflated with Pentecost. Firstfruits is supposed to be celebrated only on the 1st day of the week (Sunday) after the Sabbath during Unleavened Bread. In 1 Corinthians 15, Yeshua is the first fruit of those who have previously died, at this juncture some might say refers only to the Jews. John 4 tells us salvation is from the Jews and Revelation 22 informs us that this redemption springs from the lineage of King David. First Fruits celebrates the coming of the Messiah with the first harvest of spring crops and the 2nd planting. Notice that Firstfruits is the 2nd annual pilgrimage. It is a picture of the resurrection implying at least one additional return by the 2nd Godhead. Some might infer we can also interpret this as a type of redemption already occurring for the Old Testament Jew. Although, verse 23 clearly distinguishes another event occurring upon the Messiah's return. Could there also be a separate event to incorporate the New Testament Christian? This decision need not be determined at this juncture, but it may alter our focus to include a search for His return appearance(s). For example, it could be a terrible miscalculation to direct our attention solely to a decisive battle like Armageddon only to learn many believers were previously removed from Earth by a "rapture" event, whether Jews, Christians, or both.

Shavuot is the 4th feast. It is the Hebrew word for weeks. The event, also known as the Feast of Weeks, Festival of Harvest, Birthday of the Torah or Law, occurs during the summer month of Sivan. It is 1 of 3 festivals requiring a pilgrimage to Jerusalem. This festival celebrates the completion of the 7 weeks between Passover and Shavuot. Christians recognize the 50th day as Pentecost which is celebrated following Easter. As previously addressed, Pentecost was the event demonstrating the descent of the Holy Spirit after Yeshua's ascension. Plainly stated, the 49 days connect Passover to Pentecost through the conclusion of the Barley and Wheat Harvest. This bridges Old Testament law to New Testament grace. In other words, the story of Passover through Shavuot is the giving of the Torah, separating the righteous people from the pagans, followed by redemption. Old Testament Jewish deliverance was orchestrated through Moses while the New Testament Exodus is yet to be conducted by Jesus. The question raised is when is that Exodus or Exodus'? During these 7 weeks, 2 loaves of bread are commanded as a sacrifice reinforcing Adonai as our Lord singularly returning. Elohim is plural, written as the LORD God. Similarly, in Hebrew, the term living waters denotes a pair of lives; one life in this world and one in the world to come. Adonai represents the bread of life in this world. Genesis 3 states a man will eat bread until he returns to dust. John 6 continues this revelation when it proclaims that Jesus is the bread of life. For all who have ears let them hear.

Another view projects Passover as the engagement and Shavuot as the marriage day between God and Jewish people. If this is accurate, what are the final 3 Autumn festivals indicating? It certainly contradicts facts soon to be presented. A better question is, could these festivals represent the same religion? Are both the Jewish and Christian faith two sides of the same coin? As distasteful as this might sound to many, the evidence seems to be trending in that direction. Could this 49/50-day gap also be an indication that will occur before the next return of Christ? So far, it seems much more likely that the first 3 feasts have been adequately explained. Therefore, suggesting Passover as the engagement and Shavuot as the marriage seems highly improbable. This will be evident in the final 3 feasts yet to come. In short, our observations convey that Yeshua was crucified on Passover, buried during Unleavened Bread (which will be examined as Daniel's 70th week), and raised on Firstfruits.

Pentecost arrived after Firstfruits. Summer Pentecost brought in the fullness of Power. That fullness arrived 10 days after Jesus had already spent 40 days reunited with the disciples. Thus, Jesus ascended after 40 days, and another 10 days elapsed totaling 50 days since His resurrection. As discussed, 10 days of waiting meant the fulfillment of the law brought by the selection of a sacrificial Passover lamb. Christ's additional 40 days of teaching is the same length of time Moses spent receiving the law on Mount Sinai. Hence, the presence of the Holy Spirit replaced the need for a traditional temple building. In other words, within each person's body denotes the new sacrificial temple of God, 1 Corinthians 6. Conceivably, this completes the 3rd cycle of temples many long to see fulfilled as the first temple was destroyed in 586 B.C., and the second temple in 70 A.D. Hence, we should not insist that rebuilding another temple be required before Christ returns. If we are to consider a 4th temple, that most assuredly would come while entering the Kingdom of God.

Other notes of interest include Moses coming down from Mount Sinai when 3,000 souls were slain under God's laws. Conversely, the week after Jesus' resurrection 3,000 souls were saved. Many Jews were introduced to the "Good News" or Gospel of Grace because they were in Jerusalem for the Shavuot pilgrimage. Certainly, many millions of Christians sharing the Good News today are unknowingly part of this first Jewish harvest of three thousand souls. In Revelation 22, both the Jew and Gentile are present on each side of the river of life, 1 root with 2 tree trunks. At Pentecost, approximately 120 people were waiting in the upper room when a mighty wind came upon the disciples. Similarly, in the Old Testament, 120 priests accompanied King Solomon when the Ark of the Covenant was brought into Jerusalem, Revelation 1:6. These similarities are more than inconsequential or coincidental. They are congruent. Could this also correspond to the 120 years in Genesis? Perhaps. The guide below breaks down information from the first 4 feasts. The next chapter completes feasts 5-7 using a parallel format. Both charts present the opportunity for use as a quick reference guide to substantiate a final summation.

Feast guide 1-4:

Feast Names	Hebrew Date	Month	Length
Spring-the beginning			
1. Passover, **Pesach**, Freedom, Matzah *Barley Harvest	10th 14th	Mar-Apr Nissan-1st 1st Pilgrimage	1 day
2. Unleavened Bread Hag HaMatzot (unnamed festival)	15th-21st 21st break-through	Mar-Apr Nissan 1st Pilgrimage	7-8 days 1 week
3. First Fruits **Feast of Your Harvest**, Counting of the Omer	1st Sunday during Unleavened Bread	Mar-Apr Nissan	1 day
4. Shavuot, **Feast of Weeks, Festival of Harvest, Birthday of the Torah or Law** *Wheat Harvest	6th-7th after 7 weeks of Counting =49 days	May-June Sivan-3rd 2nd Pilgrimage	2 days

60

A FEAST TO REMEMBER

In the early years of Promise Keepers, the organization came to my hometown of Jacksonville, Florida. The downtown stadium sold tickets for this outdoor event solely for men who wanted to follow God. What happened at this service was a miracle captured on television media and newspapers alike. Others might say the news helicopters filmed a natural phenomenon, but those in attendance knew immediately what happened that day. The weather had been overcast all morning with scattered thunder showers threatening to foil the gathering. As a drizzle descended upon the heads of every man below, prayers were lifted-up by the thousands in attendance. Straight away the clouds receded only to encircle the dome structure in a barricade fashion. When the sky above had cleared, the sun shined down into the stadium like a beacon. Yet, the rain did not stop around the outside of the arena, nor did the rain enter the stadium again until the men who praised God had gone. The following day photographs captured those glorious beaming rays of sunshine. But they could not do justice to the personal testimony of those who witnessed a miracle from God that blessed day.

That was a visible manifestation of what went on inside the hearts of men in Jacksonville, Florida. My neighbor was one of those men in attendance. The next day he shared his transformative experience over the adjoining chain link fence separating our backyards. Harry began to explain how he had been held captive for years. I always knew that Harry had a disdain for certain groups of minorities even though he was a minority himself. He never felt the need to hide his displeasure with me and I never judged him for it either, though, I disagreed with his overall sentiment. Total agreement about every issue was never a requirement for us to get along. Harry was my Christian neighbor, and I considered him a friend. Instinctively I knew Christians aren't perfect people, they are meant to be a work in progress. Furthermore, his nationality had no bearing on the matter. But on this particular evening, he expressed how things had profoundly changed during the previous afternoon's visit to Promise Keepers. That was the moment Harry declared that he was free from all past prejudices. His face said it all. He was relieved. His burden was lifted, carried away by God Almighty. His exact statement, "I'm free, and I'm glad." And I was glad for him. Surely this was one of many healing stories that occurred one Saturday afternoon.

Events such as this blessed day transcend the ordinary, yet often may not seem obvious. The majority of people strive simply to survive a day-to-day routine. Though miracles may be unseen by many, they are deliberate acts of mercy and grace. They are often personal wake-up calls and momentary considerations for thanks. Whether great or small, miracles give us opportunities to offer praise and celebration. They are the proof we seek of the existence of a higher authority; a sovereign creator who is good and cares for our wellbeing. Many ordinary people clammer for such proof but reject the simple lessons all around us, every day. So many individuals ask for meaning in their lives but do not wholeheartedly search in the correct arena.

Discouragement follows closely behind unfaithfulness. The unfaithful receive no guarantees in life because they put no effort into honest action. But there is one guarantee for those willing to seek objectively and honestly. Isn't that the real question? Are people honestly inquiring for truth and understanding? Are they intentionally searching for meaning in the right arenas? For the most part, not really. Science dictates that we observe all facts in an unbiased experiment. Yet people tend to inquire on their terms, interpreting and recognizing events as they see fit to do so. We know this because most people become quite contemptuous when confronted with hard evidence contrary to their man-made thesis. Had Abram seen clouds encircle a stadium would he have assessed the situation the same as when gazing at thousands of stars scattered across a night-time sky? The evidence of a Sovereign Being has always existed. The heavens and the seasons are proof positive of a deliberate design. Abraham came to know the creator because he wanted the truth. He did not turn a deaf ear when presented with the voice of Truth. He heard the call and accepted that authority figure. Therefore, Abraham saw God as He was, faithful to complete a covenant offered. Instinctively, Abraham understood that God must be consistent and deliberate; he witnessed God's mercy and grace. Later, he would learn God's righteous judgment when dealing with Lot and Sodom. Abraham recognized that this kind of God does not change because perfection does not require improvement. All such facts are often denied today.

Thus far we have surmised how God deliberately designed seasons to distinguish the signs of the times. Within the seasons are designated feasts to symbolize events to lead a chosen people through the ages. This divine design is intended to guide all truth seekers beyond the trappings of calendars and languages through each generation. The Messiah's life finishes the 3rd set of 14 generations, through the lineage of David, Joseph, and Mary, plainly fulfilling the first 4 feasts of Passover, Unleavened Bread, Firstfruits, and Shavuot. Therefore, it seems reasonable to expect a similar fulfillment regarding the 3 remaining mainstream festivals, (excluding the Sabbath as a festival). Therefore, the search marches on toward those three... The Feasts of Trumpets, The Day of Atonement, and The Feast of Tabernacles. Will these last 3 festivals tell a story that is yet to unfold? Would we be capable of accepting or even honestly examining any future events if contrary to traditional understanding? God's appointed times await us only to be revealed like never before.

The 1st of the last 3 remaining festivals (or the 5th feast) under investigation is The Feast of Trumpets. One logical starting point would be to explore the various interpretations of the title. Examining these different names for the Feast of Trumpets may give us clues as to the implications thereof. On the left are the Jewish terms for the celebration; the right-hand column lists one or more interpretations, which appear quite revealing.

Some of the other titles:

Yom Teruah	Feast of Trumpets
	Day of (Awakening) Blasting
	Day of Shouting
Rosh Hashanah	head of the year
	birthday of the world
Teshuva	repentance
Yom HaDin	Day of Judgment
HaMelech	the Coronation of the Messiah
Yom HaZikaron	the Day of Remembrance
	Day of Memorial

Rosh Hashanah is revealed as the head of the new year, the Day of Shouting, and the Feast of Trumpets (Trumps). These interpretations become more revealing when these Jewish words are compared to New Testament scripture. Terms like Memorial and Judgment seemingly point to Revelation's Armageddon. Could this be the Day of Shouting referenced in I Thessalonians 4? Is Judgement Day different from the Day of Shouting when the 7th trumpet sounds? Will Christ receive a final victory at the beginning of our calendar year or the Jewish calendar year? Or will that occur at the head of the Jewish New Year of Tishri? Will this also be the time of Yeshua's coronation? Or will that happen after a final victorious battle? What are all these things trying to tell us? Let's begin to unpack this a few things at a time.

As expressed, Rosh Hashanah is the Hebrew name for the Feast of Trumpets. The name is derived from Leviticus 23 and Numbers 29. Rosh Hashanah is the 1st of 3 feasts taking place in the fall. It is positioned in the 7th Hebrew month called Tishrei. Therefore, Tishrei has come to be viewed as the Sabbath of the yearly calendar. Sabbatical years are calculated from the 7th month (of Tishrei). Straightaway, the significance of the number 7 presents itself to the world. For, on the 7th day of creation, God rested. We call it the Sabbath. For this reason, Tishrei is also marked as the head of the new year and the birthdate of humanity. However, Nissan is the new year for calendar months which always contains the Passover mid-way through. Rosh Hashanah is calculated 163 days after Passover by the lunar calendar hinged upon the spring equinox. Conversely, Tishrei normally corresponds to the month of September as found on the Gregorian calendar. Likewise, the Autumn Equinox always corresponds to September which aptly corresponds to the birth month of humanity.

In the New Testament, Revelation 11 signals the sounding of a final 7th trumpet which many consider to be the moment of the church rapture. In this event, all disciples will be "caught up" to meet Christ in the air, Joel 2, and I Corinthians 15. Similarly, in the Old Testament, King David returns the Ark of the Covenant and blows the shofar on the Day of the Lord, Zephaniah 1. Another interesting fact about Rosh Hashanah is that this Feast lasts 2 days. The reason why this celebration lasts 2 days is vastly overlooked. The explanation for an extra day pivoted on the uncertainty of sighting the new moon and the ability to confirm it with the Jewish court. Presently, the second day is mostly used for those outside of

Israel. Thus, if Rosh Hashanah is the day of Shouting, implying Yeshua's return, could this be a reason no one knows the day or hour of Yeshua's return, Matthew 24? Moreover, shouldn't we be considering The Feast of Trumpets as the next Biblical event instead of simply the 5th of 7 feasts? So, despite those agreeable with Christ's return, most typically disagree on the slightest date of His arrival, refusing to label any specific day or season at all. Part of this problem produces circular reasoning for those not seriously searching the scripture to at least learn the season of His return. Scripture specifically expresses that we are to know the season of His return and that no one should be ignorant. Since there are 4 seasons in a year, would it be feasible to narrow down a return within that parallel frame of 4 years? Based on the feasts and other clues, patterns will emerge from one chart to the next, chapter to chapter. Hang on for the ride.

Revisiting the supposition that Christ was born on the Feast of Trumpets which seems to have been on a Wednesday 9/11 in 3 B.C., the evidence mostly corresponds to an end time frame and a final return in 2037. Also plausible, it could simply be that Yeshua returns on the same day that the earth was created 6,000 years ago plus 40 additional years of testing.

    1997
    <u>+ 40</u>
    2037

Similarly, 2029 begins the holiday on a Sunday, also understood as the 8th day and the Firstfruits day of our Lord. So, legitimately 2029-2030 could be the year of a coming church rapture. Though the exact day of 9/11 may be less crucial than the ceremonial feast itself, here are the upcoming years that parallel dates for Rosh Hashanah, the Hebrew Head of the Year. Any one of these years could represent the coronation of Jesus.

Year	Month-day	Weekday
2026 AD	Sep/Tishri 9/11-9/13	Fri-Sun
2029 AD	Sep/Tishri 9/9-9/11	Sun-Tue
2037 AD	Sep/Tishri 9/9-9/11	Wed-Fri

The next table below lists the feasts chronologically and via the Gregorian calendar down the first column. The second column lists the feasts based on the Jewish Head of the Year. When tabling all 7 feasts side by side for comparison something interesting jumps out at the spiritually minded. The first column represents man's bird's eye view of events based upon known historical timelines. However, viewing the second column from God's perspective invites a spiritual sense. Beginning with the Feast of Trumpets we see the coronation of a King announced by the arrival of Christ. Then, the cross brings atonement for all who have sinned and professed repentance, thereby becoming dead to self. The sacrificed Jesus now requires a sacrifice, a life for a life. An eternal perspective would submit the choice of dead to self now or a 2nd death to the soul forever. By the way, this is not something anyone can repay. Hence the phrase die to self, Galatians 5. Our option to let go allows God to move within us, our Tabernacle. Ironically, the more we let go, the more whole we become. This is how pilgrims Passover into eternity and return home. Christians must ask themselves, "Am I coming clean with God?" Will we choose to see ourselves & each other as God sees us? Will we ask God his opinion? Once that happens, we can begin the process of living life more abundantly. The sky is the limit. Heaven becomes the destination, John 15. Though we strive to absolve sin, falling short is a popular theme. In fact, we seldom recognize the many ways that we fall short. The truth is, that Christians are guilty of every possible atrocity if placed in an ill-conceived situation. Once admitted, we can get over ourselves & turn over everything to God, without hanging on to any notion that anything we possess is good on our own. This is where the rubber meets the road. The world urges the idea that we can be "good" & that is enough. Instinctively, we all know this is a lie but cleave to it anyway. We cling to this thought because if we don't, the alternative means we aren't in control or at least recognize that we shouldn't be. Jesus is our ticket to freedom, our Firstfruit. We must move beyond being fans and become followers. Discipleship requires intentional action. Jesus not only improves us from where we stand currently but the Savior also delivers us from what we would have become without Him.

Lastly, the second column of Pentecost restores us spiritually through marriage. Unexpectedly, this perspective coincides with some Rabbi's interpretations of the marriage event or even the engagement to God. After marriage, the Age ends as we know it on earth. This concludes the 2nd column of feasts order. One column calls for the order of mankind. The 2nd column calls for Godly insight. For this reason, we should continuously reevaluate every aspect of our understanding, constantly striving to gain freedom from our self-imposed snares and vices. Each analysis must be evaluated solely from God's perspective lest our aim miss the bull's eye. This cannot happen without access to the Kingdom of God, spiritually. This kingdom cannot be accessed without the cross. If we cannot put down our bodies as unto death of self, we will deceive ourselves in the most unlikely arenas. Even churches proclaiming victory by His stripes overlook the scriptures of obedience unto death and suffering for the purification of the saints. If it were not so, God would have said otherwise, Philippians 2 and Hebrews 5. Christians must lean into the Spirit of God, look over His shoulder, and do as the Father does, John 5. Again, this requires revelation and steadfastness, Galatians 1.

1-7	Gregorian calendar	Hebrew calendar
1	Passover	Trumpets
2	Unleavened Bread	Atonement
3	Firstfruits	Tabernacle
4	Pentecost	Passover
5	Trumpets	Unleavened Bread
6	Atonement	Firstfruits
7	Tabernacle	Pentecost

Moreover, when observing the feasts from God's perspective events become transparent. Since God commanded observation of specific days on the Hebrew calendar, there must be a reason. Even the number 5 evokes meaning. Here we can see that the 5th feast of Rosh Hashanah mirrors grace, the "Good News" of the gospel; another reason to support this season as a harvest or being "caught up" to meet Christ.

Yom Kippur is the 6th feast. 10 days of repentance concludes by overlapping Rosh Hashanah. The 7 days linking the 2 celebrations are called the Days of Awe. This is a time of repentance and remembrance of God's promises. Disciples are to reflect on God's covenant, sovereignty, omnipresence, and faithfulness. Ideally, Yom Kippur is a period of personal evaluation and is exhibited by a 25-hour fast on the 10th day of Tishri. This Day of Atonement represents a sin offering substituting for a ritual sacrifice. Jewish prayers become a request asking God to be inscribed for another year until Yeshua's subsequent opportunity to return arrives. Christians would recognize this as written in the Book of Life for another year. If a rapture occurred on Rosh Hashanah, one might surmise that Yom Kippur may act as the prescription for a salvation extension for the following year. This may account for the inclinations of several returns until Armageddon. Revelation 3 seems to reinforce this same application. Additionally, Noah rode the storm for 1 year and 10 days. This mirrors exactly the distance between Rosh Hashanah and Yom Kippur. Noah locked the hatches 7 days before the rain. Let us hope some are not left stranded for 7 years until the next opportunity for salvation, or not at all.

In the book of Revelation God informs Yeshua to ready His return. The High Priest enters the Holy of Holies to begin the ritual process. Jesus begins the temple cleansing process involving a sin offering for the elect which takes 1 week. Is this prior to returning for Armageddon? Could this 1-week description of preparation inside the Holy of Holies equate to the 7-years after a Rosh Hashanah rapture and before God's Day of Awe, a reckoning for those in defiance? As expressed in both previous publications, 1 week converts to 7 years. Conceivably, this could be a legitimate link to a 7-year vial period of judgment known as the Great Tribulation. Accordingly, Rosh Hashanah and Yom Kippur illustrate an expectation for the Messiah to return and redeem his sheep. Will Yeshua find faith anywhere on earth upon a final rendezvous? Perhaps it is possible to ascertain exactly when these 7 vials will begin. Or are there any indications that one or more of these vials have already started?

Some believe God opens the Books of Life and Death on Rosh Hashanah only to seal those names forever on Yom Kippur. Any person failing to fast and repent will be cut off,

Leviticus 23. For this reason, Yom Kippur is also called the Day of Judgment, Joel 2. Repentance is prescribed to begin on the 1st of Elul (the 6th month) lasting 40 days through the High Holies Days ending with Yom Kippur (during the 7th month). Moses is thought to have set this example with a 3rd trip to Mount Sinai asking forgiveness for God's people. His 3rd trip lasted 40 days. Those not responding in repentance will befall the aftermath of a 7th trumpet, akin to sounding an alarm. Blowing of the shofar, or rams' horn, was also used in functions like coronating kings, convening assemblies, and announcing the Jubilee year or a new moon. Here we see several practical prospects to suggest why the 7th trumpet might be blown directly before a church rapture or even that part of the church could be redeemed on the 2nd day, meaning the following year. On a grand scale, this week of days might be considered the inverse of 7 creation days.

The trumpet may also be signaling additional information. The origins of the horn date back as a reminder of Abraham's obedience to God. The story of his son, Isaac, being spared when God provided a sacrificial ram in his stead prompts us to recognize redemptive foreshadowing. Hence, a popular tradition during Rosh Hashanah is throwing breadcrumbs into flowing water for the forgiveness of sins. Christians see Jesus Christ as the living water, the lamb sacrificed for the pardon of sin, John 4. Not coincidentally, the bread, called Challah, is round symbolizing the eternal circle of life. More specifically, up to 70 shofar blasts are made in 3 sets on the 1st day, likely representing the completion of a Sabbatical cycle of 70 years; 30 more blasts are sounded on the 2nd day, totaling 100. Is it possible that 70 may indicate Yeshua's return following the conclusion of a Sabbatical cycle or Jubilee year? Could this suggest some combination of 70 and 30 years toward future events? If so, from what points of reference might we extend the 70 and 30 years? 30 has other implications. In the Old Testament, Aaronic priests were dedicated into ministry at age 30. Likewise, Christ and John the Baptist began preaching the Gospel at age 30. Lastly, King Nebuchadnezzar II sieged Jerusalem for 30 months until the Temple of Solomon was destroyed in 587 B.C. But for now, let's assume the blasts are years beginning with the reunification of Jerusalem to be addressed momentarily.

The 7th Festival arrives on the 15th day of the 7th month, 5 days after Yom Kippur, and lasts 7 days. The Festival has several names such as Festival of Booths or Tents, Sukkot, Feast of Tabernacles, and The Ingathering. This final feast is the 3rd spiritual pilgrimage requiring all to abandon materialism. Why did God command 3 Pilgrimages? Could each pilgrimage mirror the season of Christ's return to earth? Might these 5 days between Yom Kippur and Sukkot introduce Christ's 3rd pilgrimage to Earth? Is this man's final opportunity for repentance? Is it too late? Remember 5 denotes grace and 3 denotes Christ. Perhaps Sukkot ushers in the millennium or New Jerusalem. New Jerusalem possesses 3 gates on 4 sides for a total of 12. No one enters except through these narrow gates. Jesus is the only Way, the one Savior. Of these 3 major festivals, Passover, Pentecost, and Sukkot, only Sukkot is designated as the season of our rejoicing, Isaiah 12. Each morning, synagogue services perform a Water Libation ceremony invoking God's blessing for rain. Rain represents the blessings of God through the fruit of Spiritual transformation. Nationally, Israel recognizes this feast as a time of forgiveness as demonstrated by the presentation of a 2nd set of tablets conveying the covenant. Could this act be showing completion of the 7 ages?

Sukkot also fulfills the purpose of creation, exhibiting completion. Yet, it cannot be overlooked that Sukkot is the only festival with no specific event attached. Could this be a prediction that many Hebrews would never acknowledge the first arrival of a Messiah thereby rejecting to house the Spirit of God at Pentecost? Until this void is filled, Sukkot is a picture of the Jews wandering in the wilderness living in tents until that 2nd (or even 3rd) return of salvation fully manifests. And if the Sukkot harvest represents a 2nd chance at atonement for the surviving Jews, will they finally accept

Yeshua? Since this battle is thought to destroy 1/3 of the earth, would this mimic that feasts symbolic requirement of giving up materialism for those 7 days/years? Or does it mean we give us this realm entirely?

Reexamining the 2nd set of tablets presents several other interesting possibilities of symbolism. Moses had 3 trips to Mount Sinai recorded as 40 days each. Two of those trips brought 2 sets of stone tablets with 5 laws on each. Moses is said to have rested 10 days between both trips reflecting the same 50-day interval as Pentecost. Conceivably, each tablet of laws is completed by grace to show God's mercy. Grace completes the law with the sacrifice of a Messiah and ultimately with a marriage that reunites the faithful with the Father. Perhaps this is why Sukkot is considered a celebration of double thanksgiving and reliance on God's protection. It signals the Father and Son unity. This thanksgiving may correlate to a 1 to 7-year wedding ceremonial process before returning to earth with Christ. Likewise, this marriage ceremony might indicate the same timeframe as the Great Tribulation. Could Sukkot be signaling both events at the same time? Sukkot seems to confirm that a rapture-style event must precede a 7-year time of suffering or mourning. This scenario proves believable to those who recognize that Christ saves some who come to trust in Him during the midst of the Great Tribulation. If so, they may include the Old Testament Jews since the Messianic Jew would already have risen with the New Testament church. Nevertheless, this task of finding salvation after the Spirit of God has been removed from the earth seems remote at best, if not impossible. Additionally, let's be clear, these 7-years called the Great Tribulation should not be commingled with the tribulation period of 42 months, otherwise known as the abomination of desolation. Both are completely separate periods, just as each feast is independent though interconnected. Though many still teach that the abomination has yet to come, it has already occurred and still exists on Mount Moriah today.

Circling back, if we attempt to apply the shofar blasts some interesting thoughts can be proposed. If blasts adhere to time, 70 times could be interpreted as 70 years. Hence, it is conceivable that 70 years might be used to display the season of restoration for Jerusalem. Likewise, 30 blasts could represent 30 years and be applied after the 70 blasts thereby completing a priestly ordination picture mirroring the Old Testament.

    1967 1st day
    -70   Years in blasts
    1897 First Zionist Congress

    1967 Jerusalem reunited
    +30   Years in blasts
    1997 2nd day completed

    1997 Jerusalem reunited
    + 30 Additional blasts/age Jesus starts ministry
    2027 Chabad custom

In this scenario, 3 sets of blasts on the 1st day might represent our first group of Hebrew festivals. Whether that framework constitutes traditional Old Testament Jewish learning, or the New Testament fulfillment of those feasts may be debatable. The 30 blasts on the 2nd day add more enlightenment as 1997 complements the message of completion articulated within Ussher's definition of 6,000 years from creation. Here we see that the last 100 years were prompted by the First Zionist Congress of 1897. This was considered the first official meeting to re-establish Israel as a nation. The third equation shows an additional 30 blasts as practiced by Chabad custom. Later, the year 2027 will resurface, becoming more significant.

In summation, Sukkot is 7 days of joyous celebration and the last of 3 pilgrimages to Jerusalem. It Might imply a final return to earth after a 7-year honeymoon. If so, this could equate to the end of an age. Remember, this honeymoon trip is only for those who profess Jesus of Nazareth as Lord and Christ. After capturing the Holy Site in 1967, Messianic Jews have multiplied within Israel but still only exist in drastically low population numbers based on percentages. Yet even the Messianic Jew continues to celebrate the feasts as God commanded. The lasting impression seems to be that these last 3 feasts tell a future story of a rapture event followed by destruction and subsequent rebirth. Notice that the 7 Days of Awe falls between the 7th Trumpet and Atonement for the Jews. The modern church might describe this period as "The Great Tribulation" or Armageddon. 5 more days pass before the "Ingathering," which totals 12 days. All 12 tribes and all adopted are gathered together in preparation to marry the Lamb for the next 7 years. Could these 7 years also symbolize the earth as fallow for 1 Sabbatical? Does Sukkot usher in New Jerusalem after marriage? Don't we all return with Christ after marriage? The final 3 feasts are diagramed next. The 6th month of Elul is included because it links repentance prayer to Rosh Hashanah and Yom Kippur through 40 days of prayer.

Feast guide 5-7:

Feast Names	Hebrew Date	Month	Length
(Rosh Chodesh **Elul**)	1st Elul	Aug-Sept Elul=6th	40 days
Fall 5. The Feasts of Trumpets, Rosh Hashanah, Day of Shouting/Blasting, Remembrance, Memorial, Judgment	1st or 2nd 7th Trumpet	Sept-Oct Tishri=7 Pilgrimage	1 day per Torah
6. The Day of Atonement, Yom Kippur, Repentance	10th 7 days of Awe between	Sept-Oct Tishri=7 1st Pilgrimage	25 hrs.
7. Sukkot, The Feast of Tabernacles, Booths, Tents, Ingathering	15th 5 days between	Sept-Oct 3rd Pilgrimage	7 days or 1 week

WHAT A DIFFERENCE A DAY MAKES

Over decades I have observed many believers question many of the same things. A common occurrence is that believers eventually question why most Christians don't worship on the traditional Saturday Sabbath. Of course, the answer can be approached from different vantage points, the best being that Sunday represents (Feast of) "Firstfruits" as the day Christ rose from the dead. Unfortunately, this belief is not uniformly established across Christian dogma. Some brothers from different denominations capitalize on this dogma and use it as a proselytizing tool. Having lived a long life, I have witnessed denominations testify why they possess the "right" inerrant doctrine. In such cases, they often profess loudly why all the other doctrines are "wrong." To this day, I have not found a church that is one hundred percent correct about every jot and tittle. Nor have I discovered even one that admits they are incorrect about anything specific. Regrettably, this attitude has divided the multitudes, rather than celebrate unity on the cross. Leviathan is this elusive killer. He lacks humility, especially in leadership. Moreover, pride is the main problem encompassing all of society. It hides beneath the surface only to rear its' ugly head on issues that divide the army of Christ while professing the banner of His name. One sect wears headbands advertising a weekday as if it signifies salvation. So, what difference does a day make? In the end, worshiping on Saturday or Sunday can't keep you from salvation, it certainly doesn't prevent you from praying, so it won't keep you out of heaven. But a lack of humility is another story. Blessed are the pure in heart, the meek, the humble, for they shall see God, Matthew 5. Humbleness is a necessary provision, allowing us to know the Truth.

So far, several chapters have made references concerning Sabbatical and Jubilee years. As established, Jesus was most likely born on September 11, 3 B.C. This date documented by Joseph Lenard, falls at the head of the year in the Hebrew month of Tishri 1. This date also celebrates the Feast of Trumpets, the crowning of a King. The first year of Jesus' ministry was a Sabbatical year. Whether or not this was a Jubilee year remains to be proved. Thus, the importance allocated to this Sabbatical needs to be explored further.

First, a Sabbath day refers to the 7th day of the week. The Jewish Sabbath day is Saturday. Some of the Feasts discussed also have special Sabbath days. Additionally, some years are considered Sabbatical years as well as Jubilee years. For example, earlier we mentioned each 7th year was a Sabbatical year, that God commanded the land to be at rest from cultivation. In this 7th Shemitah year, all debts were designated to be "released" or forgiven. All land and provisions were made accessible to the needy. When 7 Sabbatical years have elapsed, the ensuing year, or 50th year, is called a Jubilee year or Yovel.

> 7 years of Sabbaths = 1 Sabbatical year
> x 7 Sabbatical years
> 49 years = 1 cycle
>
> 49 years = 1 cycle
> + 1 also 1st year of next cycle
> 50th Jubilee year or Yovel

Though the Sabbatical and Jubilee Years were established in the Old Testament and certainly in Shavuot, the 49-year cycle mirrors the gap between Passover and Pentecost. In the

New Testament, scripture underscores that the 50th day ushered in the Holy Spirit. Through the power of the Holy Spirit, every believer is sanctified. Likewise, in this 50th Jubilee year, all slaves are set free, all debts are forgiven, and all lands are returned to the original Hebrew owners. However, while I believe this to be correct, there is much consternation concerning the exact year of Jubilee. Some believe it to fall on the 49th year, while others insist it arrives the following year. Still, others suggest that, under certain circumstances, an additional year of Jubilee beyond the 50th has merit. Due to the repetitive context of the number 50 and the fact that the word Jubilee means 50, it seems logical to conclude that it means what it says. In other words, the 50th year is the Jubilee year. It also qualifies as the 1st year of the next Sabbatical cycle of 49, as declared in Leviticus 25. In this way, the integrity of the 7 cycles is maintained. More evidence for this will be examined for further support. Still, the question remaining herein is what sequence of 49 years marks the beginning of a Jubilee on our current calendar? This discovery may prove difficult since most of the original documentation was lost when the Jews were exiled around 722 B.C. So, our search will need to hinge on additional events for more answers. But, because these dilemmas persist, it could also be another reason why the exact return date of Christ could be considered a persistent mystery. That is to say, if Christ represents the redemptive nature of the Jubilee, itself.

Tackling a definitive Jubilee cycle will be difficult for several other reasons. First, it wasn't consistently observed by all Jewish people. Furthermore, this was exacerbated during the Second Temple period as many Jews lived outside Israel so there was no real commitment to adhere to this extra standard. Third, other civilizations would never agree to return land purchased in a transaction simply because someone else's religion required them to do so. This religious implication toward non-Jewish nations alone seemingly justified this celebratory omission. Besides, all twelve tribes were never fully restored within their individually Godly assigned territories. Thankfully, Leviticus 25 plainly states that a Jubilee Year starts on the Day of Atonement giving us some direction. Today, Israel begins the Sabbatical Year on the Jewish New Year, Tishri 1, and celebrates the Day of Atonement on Tishri 10. Soundly, evaluating both dates on a Jubilee cycle we can determine the last Sabbatical year extends 1 year, 10 days. Remarkably, this mirrors the same length Noah was secured inside the Ark, Genesis 7-8. Since Yeshua is our Atonement for sin, He is also the manifestation of the Ark of the covenant. Could this 1 year, 10 days be a signal to New Testament believers as well? To extrapolate, will the raptured saints be in heaven for 1 year and 10 days until the Messiah descends again for final vengeance upon the earth? Or is there another return yet undiscovered? Is the extra 10 days significant in that it leads to the Day of Atonement opportunity for non-Jesus-believing Jews after the 1st rapture? This does seem to endorse those previously suggested conclusions. Furthermore, couldn't this scenario place Christians and Jews who are still living on earth well into the thick of the final days of tribulation? Wouldn't this be contrary to most seminary teaching and therefore rejected immediately out of hand by most modern-day theologians? It is time to reexamine these days and refocus on other aspects of Noah that might have been overlooked.

Even though the phrase is often misused, the Hebrews were God's chosen people. This fact never absolved the Jewish people from punishment. For example, God's chosen were delivered into exile for 70 years. This number was not arbitrarily assessed; 70 years accounted for 49 cycles x 10 or 490 years when they profusely omitted observances of the Sabbath as reported in Jeremiah 25. Notice that God must punish all people for disobedience according to the law.

Jesus reiterates this reasoning in Matthew 18 when answering the concept of forgiveness as 70 x 7. In other words, forgive one another indefinitely until the Jubilee cycle becomes everlasting. (Believers are commanded to be in a perpetual cycle of forgiveness if they want to be above the law wrapped in grace. However, this does not excuse us from abiding by the law. Obedience is required for discipleship.) In Numbers 11 Moses selects 70 elders demonstrating a like-minded spiritual sense of order and completeness. Those same 70 elders presented themselves to Moses at Mount Sinai pleading their case for him to return for a second set of tablets, Exodus 24. Also, in the book of Psalms chapter 90, a generation lasts 70 years plus as many as 10 more. Could these 70 years plus 10 help narrow the window of Christ's return? These questions will be revisited to assist in making that determination.

Historian Josephus recorded Sabbatical and Jubilee years encompassing the birth of Christ. For example, he recorded Herod's conquest of Jerusalem on the Day of Atonement in 37-36 B.C. By definition, this was another incidence of Israel's Judgments. Herod reigned another 34 years after the death of Antigonus, who perished soon after Jerusalem's defeat. This places Herod's death around 1 B.C., rather than the commonly presupposed norm several years earlier. Herod's decree to kill all unborn male babies under the age of 2 aligns with the current thesis that Yeshua was born in 3 B.C. Moreover, if the Magi traveled 2-1 B.C., they would have been free to do so if it was during a Sabbatical Year. Those traveling outside Jerusalem would have an extra year as well.

Next are several construction projects and historical events documented during the Sabbatical Years.

Caesarea Philippi	2 B.C. – 1 B.C.
Jesus' ministry begins	27 A.D. – 28 A.D.
Jerusalem's Northern third wall	41 A.D. – 42 A.D.
Rebuilding Caesarea Philippi	62 A.D. – 63 A.D.
Jerusalem's Temple destroyed	69 A.D. – 70 A.D.
Jewish Revolt v. Romans	132 A.D. – 133 A.D.

Building projects during a Sabbatical Year makes perfect sense because unused labor would be abundant. These building projects give credibility and support this research thus far. But perhaps we should take another step back into scripture for re-examination. By investigating Daniel's 70 weeks, is it possible to determine if his prophecy was given in Sabbatical Years? If this is the case, Daniel 9:24-27 must tell us more than just the arrival of an "Anointed One." Thus, it might not just be a link forward to the Messiah's birth but also become a conduit to His final appearance. This deserves serious investigation, if we want to discover where we stand in history's timeline.

First, breaking down the calculation of weeks requires remembering the feasts are based on the Jewish lunar calendar. Therefore, 12 months of 30 days each equals a year consisting of 360 days (just as expressed in the day of Noah,

Genesis 7 and 8). Logically, a week of 7 days converts to 7 years. The total time supplied in Daniel is 70. Multiplying 7 times 70 equals 490. This is the Jubilee cycle. However, Daniel distinguishes those weeks by parts 69 and 62 weeks. This separates 7 weeks until the Messiah is to be "cut off." Could this separation of years indicate a 49-year hidden Jubilee cycle? Mathematically, somewhere during these 70 weeks must contain at least one complete Jubilee period. Ben Zion Wacholder investigated that conviction. Ben uses the decree of King Cyrus which ends Jewish captivity, and rebuilds Jerusalem and the Temple, Isaiah 44:28. Josephus confirms the rebuilding in his book "Antiquities." In addition, Tim Warner states some theologians believe King Cyrus' decree fell on the 70th Jubilee from creation. However, the creation date (or even the fall date) might be one additional Sabbatical and is not our pressing concern. Nonetheless, the most plausible reasons Daniel divides the timeline into 69 and 62 weeks is to distinguish the Sabbatical, a Jubilee, Unleavened Bread, or possibly an additional 8th cycle. Naturally, 7 Sabbaticals and 1 Jubilee would fall during these 49 weeks and the 8th cycle could consist of the 70th week. Reviewing previous charts reminds us that Methuselah was the 8th generation born from creation (the name translated as bringing death). Enoch was the 7th generation. His name means teacher. Therefore, 7 represents a rabbi bringing completion. Enoch was one of two in the Old Testament who rose to meet God in the air without dying. This foreshadowed Yeshua's finished work at the cross and ascension 40 days following the resurrection.

This first 7-week Sabbatical period also identifies with the last book of Nehemiah, known as the silent period. God delivered a final message through Malachi, completed in around 397 B.C., which began approximately 400 years of silence. Most theologians agree the sealed period ended with the birth of John the Baptist in 4 B.C. Incidentally, John was born approximately 6 months before Jesus and paved the way for the Truth in baptism. Likewise, it is plausible that the final 7th seal would include the birth of Christ in 3 B.C. and progress through His death and resurrection, extending another 33 years. In any case, Daniel, Nehemiah, and Malachi all submit evidence that the sealed times are ending, and the good news will be extended unto the Gentiles. This theme is confirmed within the context of Daniel's 70 weeks and the proper interpretation is long overdue. Adding 69 weeks of 7's from the decree of King Cyrus should bring us to the cross and resurrection of the "Anointed One."

7 weeks	69-62 weeks
x 7 years	1 Sabbatical
49 years	1 cycle
62 weeks	Divided by Daniel
x 7 years	1 Sabbatical
434 years	Jubilee 435th
434 years	7 Sabbaticals
+49 years	69th week
483 years	Messiah "cut off" - Jubilee 484th

The glaring question needs to be addressed. If religious leaders had foreknowledge of a Messiah, why did they miss Yeshua's arrival? They were perfectly capable of figuring out this mathematical calculation. Daniel delivered the season, but it was hidden from their sight. Furthermore, the good news of the Gospel was to be concealed until after the crucifixion work was "finished" and the resurrection to life everlasting was revealed. Plainly stated, this was the final 7th seal referred to during the silent period and mentioned in my previous two books. All the seals were kept quiet until the coronation of the King. Once the trumpets announced the arrival of the Kingdom of God, all spiritual eyes would be opened. Those trapped by unbelief or dogma cannot see it.

Ben Zion Wacholder breaks down his idea of the 69 weeks marked after King Cyrus issues "his decree (in 3502 AM = 461/460 B.C.) the Messiah would be "cut off." This would be after 3985 AM (3502 + 483 years = 3985 AM or 23/24 AD). Wacholder seems to solidify the view that the remaining 70th week occurred through the final 7 years of the crucifixion in 30 A.D. This may or may not imply the final week to be "cut off" midway through the cycle. Nevertheless, Wacholder aligns with previous assumptions that Jesus began His ministry in about 27 A.D. at the precipice of a Sabbatical Year, also called a Shmita year. According to Daniel, the 70th year may have been the 8th week. This supposes the dividing times of 62 and 69 indicate a Jubilee cycle. In short, this places Jesus's ministry during the 1st week of a Shmita Sabbatical cycle. We also know the end of Yeshua's ministry aligned with a festival. Perhaps this is what Paul purported in 1st Corinthians 15 when he called Jesus the First Fruits (festival) of those who have fallen asleep. Remarkably, this reinforces the spiritual feasts in the 2nd column previously charted.

Lastly, this decree also ties to our supposition that Jesus began His ministry around 30 years of age, placing a logical birthdate of approximately September, 3 B.C. Revelation 2 supports this year and seasonal claim as it describes the sun and moon relative to the constellation of Virgo which appeared briefly on the September equinox. Underscoring this realization, we should not take such phrases lightly that instruct us to know the season of His return. This reinforces the significance of the Hebrew word for seasons, Moed, which means, "appointed times." Reconstructing the Rabbi's model, we see the dates are slightly askew. Notwithstanding, the Rabbi's dates may have accidentally predicted another event yet to be stumbled upon. That revelation comes much later in this saga. Below is the missing cutoff week based on the Jewish Head of the Year calendar.

27/28 A.D. Sabbatical year
28/29 A.D. Extra Sabbatical year
29/30 A.D. Likely no Extra Jubilee year
30 A.D Next Sabbatical "Cut off" by crucifixion

Another assessment using our presupposed Sabbatical dates allows us to reconstruct a logical 70th week when the Messiah is "cut off" mid-way through the final 7-year cycle. This view connects the final 7-year cycle by bisecting two 3½ years periods while aligning with historical records regarding the destruction of the 2nd temple in 69/70 A.D. Daniel's 70-week prophecy is an entirely different matter.

483 years = 69 weeks x 7
-26/7 A.D.
457/8 B.C. Daniel's prophecy

27 A.D. Shmita Sabbatical
+ 3 ½ Sabbatical ½ cycle
30 A.D. Cross and resurrection
+ 3 ½ Sabbatical ½ cycle
34 A.D. Next Sabbatical

Sabbatical years by historical construction:

41/42 A.D. Jerusalem's Northern third wall
48/49 A.D. Sabbatical Year
55/56 A.D. Sabbatical Year
62/63 A.D. Rebuilding Caesarea Philippi
69/70 A.D. Temple destroyed 6-8th Sabbatical

To be clear, Christ's ministry does not appear to include a Jubilee year. Until now, the precise Jubilee dilemma could not be definitively proven. A recently discovered ancient Babylonian tablet called VAT 4956 possessed the last key to resolving this lingering impasse. Londo Mollari presents the evidence contained within chronicles as the destruction of Jerusalem and Jewish captivity popularly found within Jeremiah 52. Through a series of inscribed dates from VAT 4956 (as well as other tablets and records) and Stellarium software, he quantifies the validity of the tablets. For example, if the information indicates the 37th year of King Nebuchadnezzar as 568-567 B.C., the 18th year of Hebrew captivity is 587 B.C. Then, it is feasible to determine the Babylonian King's first year of reign as 604 B.C. From this data, the calculation can be confirmed with the fall of Jerusalem in scripture.

    567   37th year of Nebuchadnezzar II
  + 37   years of reign
    604   1st regnal year

    567   37th year of Nebuchadnezzar II
  + 18   18th year captives from 2nd siege
    587   Jerusalem falls

With this information, Nick Vanderlaan is thought to have uncovered the Jubilee year lost during the Babylonian captivity. First, Nick calculates the 7th-year date of captives in Jeremiah by using the figures from Mollari's work above. The final step adds 25 years to the first year of King Jehoiachin's captivity which is also the 14th year after the destruction of Jerusalem from the book of Jeremiah.

    587   Jerusalem falls
  + 11   18th year captives from 2nd siege
    598   7th year captives from 1st siege

598   1st year of King Jehoiachin
+ 25   Exiled 12th month, 1st year
574-3   Jubilee

587   Jerusalem falls
+ 14   Ezekiel 40
574-3   *Jubilee confirmed

574-3 B.C. seems most impressive and irrefutable. That date correlates spot-on, with the Israelite's entrance into the Holy Land in 1406-1407 B.C. Consequently, the beginning era of a Jubilee should begin within a year. In addition, both previous calculations are within one year of each other regarding the first Sabbatical year of Yeshua's ministry. However, the latter indicates that Sabbatical may be one or two years off moving forward from Babylonian captivity depending on one's interpretation of scripture. This discrepancy surfaces again when comparing Josephus' building projects with the Sabbatical years surrounding the era of Christ's life on Earth. Notwithstanding, what if Josephus did not possess the correct Jubilee dates as well? Perhaps he made an educated guess regarding an actual Sabbatical year or based it upon approximate Rabbinical knowledge of his day. Of course, during this period Josephus would have recorded building projects using a Roman calendar, not a Jewish timeline. Just as conflict arose between the Babylonian dating system and the Israelite system, so could be part of the cause of another discrepancy here. Assuming the accuracy of supporting information that 27 A.D. or 28 A.D. is a Shmita Year, our attention can be focused on addressing the Sabbatical cycles moving forward. By interjecting Jubilee years, we can hope to discover potential seasonal relevance within our current century. In that vein, let's speed up the process by using larger cycle increments.

Jubilee guide from Christ:

15-16 A.D.	Vanderlaan Jubilee	0 + 1 A.D.	7/7
27-28 AD	Suggested Shmita	Christ ministry begins	2-3/7 Shmita
28-29 AD	Vanderlaan Shmita		
62-63	*Suggested Shmita	*Aligns Josephus 69 A.D.	*8th
64-65	Vanderlaan Jubilee		7/7
554-555	Jubilee	49 x 10	7/7
1044-1045	Jubilee	49 x 10	7/7
1534-1535	Jubilee	49 x 10	7/7
2024-2025	Vanderlaan Jubilee & his rapture belief	49 x 10	70th Jubilee from Exodus
2023-2030	*1-2 Rapture + 4-7 years	Temple *70 AD	*8th week
2030-2037	Post Apocalypse	*14th year	7 years
1988-2037	Millennium - New Jerusalem	President Prophecy	7x7=49

Shockingly, while Daniel's 70 weeks have led to us the birth of Christ, this recently discovered Jubilee may have also led us to His return. According to Vanderlaan that time is 2024-2025. He bases that model on Daniel's 70 weeks converted to Jubilees. Roger Young estimated 1407-1406 B.C. as the date of Joshua's crossing over the Jordan River. This confirms that 70 Jubilees have indeed passed until 10/2-4/2024. Below is a chart based on Usher's 4004 B.C. year of creation. Incredibly, it confirms the identical Jubilee scriptures that the above chart claims. The sequence of the exact final tribulation could vary but the pretribulation rapture prescription remains within a very tight 7-year window on or after Rosh Hashanah 2024. These additional 4-7 years represent a novel thesis suggesting the time elapsed while living inside the Garden of Eden. Those days are reapplied to the last Jubilee date of 2024 as one possibility of extending the pretribulation year.

Jubilee guide from Creation:

4004 BCE	Usher's Creation	Jubilees	Years
(4000-3997 B.C.)	Garden ex-communication	+ -	*4-7
1554-3 B.C.	*14th year Jacob marries Leah Joseph was 8	50	2450
1407-6 B.C.	Israelites cross the Jordan River	53 (3)	2597 (147)
574-3 B.C.	*14th year after Babylonian exile	70 70-53=17	3430

		120	
1876-7 AD	50th from exile		5880
2024-5 AD	70th Jubilee after Crossing Jordan Vanderlaan's date	123 (Next 3)	6027 (147)
2023-2030	Pre-Tribulation	69-70 AD	*8th week
2030-2037	2-week mirror	14-28 AD	2x7=14

According to these determining factors, the Messiah's return is most likely to occur on one of the days during the annual Rosh Hashanah feast. Thus, we know the season. But can we know the year or even the actual day or hour? Well, maybe not the day or hour. One step at a time. But the timing of the shock and awesome tribulation, "Day of Atonement," becomes less significant if a rapture has already happened. Although, some believe this last phase of tribulation offers a 2nd chance at redemption. It seems to imply at least one more Sabbatical.

What piques my interest concerning this chart is the 1988 A.D. Sabbatical Year. This is the year I received my Word from God expressed in "Seer in the Way." The message was delivered following the 40th year of Israel's national rebirth, a Sabbatical Year. The remaining time in question from my book leaves a 49-year gap needing context. Now, we can verify the gap is identified as a Sabbatical Year arriving in 2037 A.D. Though not a documented Jubilee year, the sum of years is equivalent to a Sabbatical cycle with 2038 representing the 50th year; 2038 also qualifies as the 8th year and the 1st year of the following Sabbatical cycle.

> 1948 Israel re-established
> + 40 Woman purification days & mirrors crossing
> 1988 Year notated in "Seer in the Way"
>
> 1988 No more time notated
> + 49 Unknown cycle notated in "Seer in the Way"
> 2037 Age ends

Rabbi Davidson endorses 2028-2029 as the next Sabbatical year disagreeing with the current proof. Knowing the Jubilee falls in 2024-2025 we can be certain that the next Sabbatical arrives in 2030. However, 2029-2030 could also be considered the 8th week which brings destruction. This 8th-week supposition aligns with the destruction date of the temple, generally agreed to have occurred in 69-70 A.D., as noted by Josephus. Does this 8th week imply the removal of God's 3rd temple, meaning the elect? Is 2030 the marker of destruction for humanity? Or does destruction come 7 years after being "caught up" to meet God? Regardless, the window of a rapture event has now been reduced within 7 years by several different angles. To press further, more revelation is paramount. Just as Peter received revelation from the Father in heaven that Jesus was the Anointed One, in this same way some come to know the day of His coronation. Those who are unprepared will have their moment stolen like a thief during the darkest hours. While most of Mathew 24 has already been documented by <u>Seer in the Way</u>, that specific faithful day has not been accurately tested until now. For some, it may be helpful to remember that the Magi were only a select minority who knew a Messiah was born. Almost all of the Jewish Rabbis were as surprised as everyone else. In this vain, shall the educated leadership of our day also discount

Yeshua's season. The proof is already before us. Christians dismiss the very idea of obeying feast commandments.

How can we be as sure as the Magi that Jesus comes at the Moed? Because God is order. He composed mathematical principles that govern the universe. He uses seasons and events as reference points that defy calendars. Surmising 1948 A.D. as the re-establishment for the nation of Israel is a logical end-time signal for us to acknowledge. This sets off alarm bells, especially for the opposition. Is it a coincidence that 1948 A.D. plus 7 Sabbatical years brings us to 1997 A.D., equaling 6000 years of creation?

    1948 Israel nationhood
    + 49 7 Sabbatical Years
    1997 6,000 years

Examining Jerusalem's reunification date via the Six-Day War of 1967, a bigger picture takes view. By subtracting 70 years we arrive at 1897 A.D., which began the "First Zionist Congress." This first congress pushed for the formation of the tiny nation of Israel to be reborn.

    1967 Jerusalem reunited
    - 70 10 Sabbaticals = 10th Noah's flood
    1897 First Zionist Congress

Likewise, the 1917 A.D. Balfour Declaration can be linked to Israel's reunification in 1967 A.D. by adding 50 years or 1 Jubilee period.

    1917 British support for Israel's nationhood
    + 50 1 Jubilee
    1967 8th day/Six-Day War

For this tiny nation to arise it first required the fall of the Ottoman Empire. Once WW II had forced the Turks to release all claims on Levant Godly nations organized a body of United Nations and spearheaded the Zionist cause. English and French forces prevailed at the Battle of Megiddo over Ottoman and German troops in 1918. Then, the "Great War" invited a 2nd world war. World War II brought a Revelation flood-like disaster upon all nations such as the world has never seen. But for the Jew, a maniacal tyrant sought to chase after them specifically as if to eradicate them from the face of the earth. This same spirit has been revived today by verbalizing the identical context, "From the river to the sea." Could this flood of vengeance be likened to the 10th generation of Noah's flood? 10 represents man's day (6) in earth's creation (4) and his responsibilities under law and order. In addition, Noah was the 8th survivor couped up inside an ark. During WW II, surviving Jews endured 8 long years of concentration camps. Was this the Jewish penance for denying Emmanuel, the New Testament Word of God? Were the unfaithful punished as well?

Dates in various chapters are beginning to connect and the relationship between events, Sabbaticals, and Jubilee Years can no longer be coincidental. Sometimes God deals with blocks of Sabbatical cycles composed of 49 (7 x 7) and 70 (7 x 10) years. This chapter accounts for all 70 weeks of Daniel's prophecy. Contextually, all 70 weeks were purposely delivered as a block of sequential years targeted to reveal the birthdate of the Messiah. According to the scripture, when Christ died on the cross the tribulation followed after the 70th week. This was covered in the book series. Applying this data logically brings a corrected perspective causing reasonably minded people to re-examine current theological gaps that jump over centuries. Whatever the duration of the last few years of the "Great Tribulation," it must be proven elsewhere.

Nevertheless, the 8th day (or Sabbatical week) and the Jewish feasts, imply an additional 7-year period after at least one rapture event. However, further evidence is needed to substantiate this claim. Thankfully, the Jubilee has been identified and logged as 70 cycles from the Jordan River crossing, arriving in 2024-2025. Will this be the year God wipes away every tear? What will happen when the full knowledge of God's plan is revealed? …That day the elect will realize they elected to participate in this universe. They were sealed the entire time, predestined. That is the day faith and death will be no more. Only love endures into the everlasting. The Hourglass commenced in 1988. We are participating in the last Jubilee.

NOT IN MY TOWN

A prophet is not accepted in his hometown, Luke 4:24. Jesus made this statement as a matter of fact and a measure of faith. This is not to suggest that faith is the sole component necessary to produce miracles. God needs no outside inputs should providence or action be taken. Thankfully, God listens to prayer, but even that does not always place the burden on faith. Scripture instructs followers who lack faith to ask for increase. Furthermore, as Christ is the author and finisher of faith, we cannot take credit for any amounts of faithful inputs we house within our temple body. Nor should we blame others for their lack of faith.

As for prophecy, certain theologians subscribe to the belief that the gift of prophecy has become obsolete with the completion of the New Testament. This narrow stance singlehandedly eliminates every prophet that may threaten church leadership. But God's gifts haven't changed yet, and neither has human nature. Just as the disciples received the delivery of gifts through the Holy Spirit, so too can we. Gifts of all types operate from the Holy Spirit today, though they continue to be denied largely by those who are intimidated the greatest. Those same leaders are likely to profess Deuteronomy 18:22, which states if a prophecy does not come to pass it did not come from God. They rarely address New Testament prophecies that actually do come to pass. Nor, do they consider other possibilities about prophecy like a stay of judgment, Exodus 32:14. Consequently, the church has expanded upon the ideas of excluding hometown prophets to prohibiting a prophet in every town. As if that is not alarming enough, by their reasoning anything not already found in scripture cannot be attributed to the "Truth" of the Gospel. Therefore, any "new revelation" is judged heretical never mind Act 2. While this may seem reasonable to some at first glance, it presents limitations to our measure of faith and understanding, not to mention living life more abundantly. From this, we can link how prophecy builds faith. And, we understand how denying the gifts of the Spirit can undermine confidence.

Most would agree that living according to scripture is the right approach, but what do we profess is the right interpretation of each verse? This is where the rubber meets the road for many well-intentioned denominations. Jesus encounters various quizzers attempting to trip him up on several occasions concerning marriage, He answers but brings to light their lack of knowledge and understanding of the scriptures as well as the kingdom of heaven. Within some responses, Jesus mentions that marriage does not occur in heaven as people become like angels, Matthew 22. Yet, Revelation 19 reveals that all believers marry the Messiah. Marriage in heaven belongs to Christ for the sole purpose of unity with the Father. Thus, the choice to marry another is not an option in heaven. Our journey home reunites us as one. That is our reward through Christ. Falsities are exposed by persistence when the Spirit leads.

Though the scripture may present an all-inclusive guide while journeying through this realm there should not exist any grandiose notion that we possess all the contents of information. By doing so, we attempt to control outcomes and people. We place ourselves on the throne. We feed our vanity disguised in Leviathan dressing. Individuals are to live each day in and by the Spirit of God. Daily revelation and discernment cannot be a trivial point. Otherwise, Jesus encounters would have been omitted from scripture altogether. Will we continue to be limited by these prejudices? At a minimum, our takeaway should display a prophetic pause when presented with the immeasurable knowledge surrounding the kingdom of God. On the other hand, scripture indicates there will always be plenty of self-proclaimed false prophets until the Messiah returns. To be clear, this acknowledgment of false prophets does not place a stamp of approval upon them, rather it recognizes their existence. Likewise, logic requires us not to ignore the implications of the declaration. Follow this reasoning:

> Logically, there will be Godly prophets right up until the Messiah returns if for no other reason than scripture warns us about false prophets.

If all the ensuing prophets after the Bible was completed were fake, we certainly wouldn't need to be warned they were coming. The scripture would only need to state plainly that all gifts of prophecy had ceased. Everyone proclaiming to be a prophet would easily be identified as a liar. This, alone, testifies that genuine prophets really do exist. So, let's not throw the baby out with the bath water. Let the preachers preach. Let the prophets prophesy. Let the Holy Spirit move as He wills. Attempting to control the fruits of those blessings results in weakness of the body. Let us not continue to be limited by our prejudices.

Ironically, the absence of New Testament prophets would also present a major problem for Judaism. Although, from a Jewish perspective this argument seems highly implausible. Centuries ago, there was a stunning prophecy revealing the nation of Israel. In 1217 A.D., Rabbi Judah ben Samuel (Judah he-Hasid) predicted the Ottoman Empire would rule over Jerusalem for 8 Jubilees. Another 300 years would pass until the Turks successfully invaded Levant in 1516-1517 A.D. In this context, a Jubilee is defined as 50 independent years separate from the Exodus event. Rabbi Judah correctly interprets the calculation as follows:

50 years	Independent
x 8 cycles	of Jubilees
400 years	Prophecy
400 years	8 Jubilees
+1517 A.D.	Ottoman rule
1917 A.D.	End of occupation

It must be noted that while the Ottoman Turks controlled Levant until 1917 A.D., they temporarily lost control of Jerusalem for 9 years. During those 9 years, an Egyptian Caliphate ruled the area. Since both occupiers were considered Islamic Caliphates, the sum is 400 years. Thus, Seljuk Turks tormented Jerusalem for 391 years, as stated in Revelation 9:15. Below is a summary calculation converted from days into prophetic years as stated in scripture and indicated in my previous two books.

360 years	1 year is 360 days = 360 years
+30 years	1 month is 30 days = 30 years
+ 1 year	1 day is 1 year
+ 15 days	360 days ÷ 24 hours In a day
391 prophetic years, 15 days	

391 prophetic years, 15 days
+9 years Egyptian conquest
=400 years of Muslim occupation

In this context, Rabbi Judah's prophecy and the book of Revelation can be considered to have concluded the same outcome of Muslim occupation. Yet, the prophetic word by Rabbi Judah did not end there. He articulated that after the Ottoman occupation ended there would be rest over the land for 1 Jubilee, the 9th. This signaled that the Ottoman Empire's reign ended on the 8th Jubilee. This could imply that the 10th Jubilee ushers in the Messianic end-time. Remember, the Old Testament tells us the mirror of Moses was also the 10th generation. However, it is additionally likely that this 10th Jubilee parallels Ismael's 10 Muslim Empires, or even the 10 Persian Empires of this 1967 era as explained in greater detail by both previous books. 2017 brings further significance that will be elaborated on in a future chapter.

    1917   Land rests after 8 Jubilees
    + 50   Fallow 1 Jubilee
    1967   End of 9th

    1967   Jerusalem restored
    + 50   10th Jubilee
    2017   *Jerusalem recognized

As predetermined, 2017 does not land on the correct historical Jubilee date of 2024-2025. 2017 engages the prior 6th cycle of the Sabbatical. Remember the 2nd temple in 69-70 A.D. was brought down the following 7th Sabbatical. This context signals the 2nd Yom Kippur War of 2023-2024 A.D. Notwithstanding, careful discernment of Deuteronomy 23 supports the 10th generational claims and backs into confirming 1967 as the correct pivot date for that final era to commence. Rabbi Judah rightly points out 400 years of Muslim rule until the land of Levant was to become fallow for 50 years. Could this be considered the New Testament counterpart to the 400 years of silence until revived by the Good News of the Gospel? If so, it is the reason why this book could not have been written before 2017. The period also mirrors the Old Testament Israelites in Egyptian bondage for 400 years, Gen 15:13. One glaring observation about Rabbi Judah is that he does not count the fallow years as a Jubilee. Therefore, if we continue with his prediction one additional cycle it brings us to his 10th Jubilee. In this scenario, Rabbi Judah expects the Messiah to return within the 50-year window 2017-2067. However, skipping periods creates other issues, just as skipping time in Daniel's prophecy did.

    2017 10th/11th Jubilee begins
    + 50 Beginning of end times
    2067 10th/11th Jubilee ends

A better representation is the generational introduction after 1967 introduced in previous books. Using either a 70-year or 100-year generational perspective will support this window of a second coming.

    1967   Jerusalem reunited
    + 100 Generation, Genesis 15
    2067   Jubilee ends/generation ends

    1967   Jerusalem reunited
    + 70   Generation Psalms 90
    2037   Possible conclusion

In this instance, it is important to remember the premise on which the 70 Sabbatical Years started. Daniel instructs us to use this perspective to detect the birth of a Messiah. Consequently, Psalms usage of 70 years for a generation carries more weight. Furthermore, Psalms is a book of prayer, protection, and deliverance. Without prayer, no one can continually act in faithfulness. They will become detached and fall into pridefulness. Then, sin and tribulations readily enter one's life "cutting off" communion with God. Applying this discovery to Israel's Independence Day is also plausible if extended by 10 years, Psalms 90.

    1948   Jerusalem reunited
    + 70   Generation Psalms 90:10
    2018   Great Tribulation

> 2018   Great Tribulation
> + 10   Tribulation extended
> 2028   Judgment & rapture

Other Rabbis besides Judah ben Samuel are thought to have contributed to prophecy illuminating the Messiah's future appearance. Whether that appearance is the 1st or 2nd occurrence depends on one's persuasion. Rabbi Eliyahu prophesied that the Hurva Synagogue would be rebuilt 3 times before Yeshua's appearance. The 3rd re-constructed temple was dedicated on March 15, 2010. Before Rabbi Eliyahu died in 1797, he went on to predict that Russia would capture Crimea and eventually infiltrate Istanbul. Crimea was captured in 1856 and 2014. It has a history of conflict and is mentioned in my previous book, "Seer in the Way." Nevertheless, Rabbi Eliyahu's prophecy makes sense in that Russia may decide to occupy Istanbul to secure permanent waterway access. Istanbul controls waterway access into Crimea. If this access were to involve force, it would become a seriously sticky situation since Turkey is currently a member of the United Nations, albeit, an often-uncooperative element. At present, Russians are welcome in Istanbul without a Visa. This has invited an influx of Russian males who are escaping the ongoing Crimean War.

Addressing the idea of a 3rd temple promotes several areas worthy of thought. First, indeed a 3rd temple of Hurva was raised. That alone is a surety. Nonetheless, it evokes ideas of a 3rd Synagogue thought required to be rebuilt on the Temple Mount before the return of Christ. As mentioned, two Mosques are currently positioned approximately where Solomon's Temple once stood. Although it is not unfathomable to propose that the current Mosques might be destroyed by war or terrorism and that a 3rd Jewish prefabricated Temple could be erected almost overnight, it may not happen until the last year and ten days, prior to the

Lord's final entry. More to the point, Pentecost brought the 3rd temple located within us represented by the Holy Spirit. Therefore, it seems reasonable that until God removes His current Spirit temple, He will not allow another erected third Jewish temple. Again, the glaring truth is that a 3rd temple of abomination has been standing for over 1260 years. The fact that this desolation goes unrecognized continues to be a major obstacle in understanding the timing of prophecy fulfillment.

As this latest declaration of abomination will likely seem overly dramatic or even ridiculous to many readers, it becomes important to retrace these footsteps. It will also undergird our current position. Restated, Revelation 12 tells the story of the Twelve Tribes of Israel disbanding and reforming as a nation. The opposition seeks to devour her, preventing the formation thereof for one thousand, two-hundred, 60 days. Since we have the luxury of already establishing Israel's national independence as 1948, we can work backwards. Subtracting 1260 years from 1948 brings us to 688 A.D.

1260	Prophecy
-1948	Nationhood
688 A.D.	1st mosque

Knowing 1967 is also a pivotal date, we can subtract another thousand, two-hundred, 60 days from 1967 to arrive at a second possible marker. Subtracting 1260 years from 1967 brings us to 707 A.D.

1260	Prophecy
-1967	Jerusalem restored
707 A.D.	2nd mosque

Whoever ruled Jerusalem during this timeframe 688 A.D. - 707 A.D., must have created an abomination of desolation referred to in Daniel 11 and Revelation 11.

Undeniable proof documents that the Umayyad Caliphate, 661-750, invaded the area and constructed the Dome of the Rock. A second mosque, Al-Aqṣā was later completed on the grounds, within sight of each other. Both Islamic structures are located within the outer court of the Jewish holy site. For additional verification, read both prior books.

What has not garnered enough verifiable consideration is the underlying theme that develops during this presentation of 1260 years. There are, in fact, 2 halves of 2520 years, both equaling 1260 years. The first half of the prophecy extends from King Nebuchadnezzar's Babylon to the Umayyad Caliphate. The second half of 1260 years is a continuation of Muslim occupation and the eventual national establishment of Israel. To this point in scripture, prophetic years have been expressed as days. The theme changes when normal prophetic days become substituted for months. For example, the length of 1260 days seems to be equivalent to the newer expression of 42 months. Yet, if they are congruent, why make a distinction? The distinction of days or months addresses the context. God's times are expressed as days to be interpreted as years. Months belong to deception and death. The identical timeframe expressed as **42 months from abomination to Israel represents an ungodly duration.** Thus, 42 represents not only deceit, destruction, and death, but more appropriately the second death.

42	Ungodly months
x 30	Days per month
1260	Days=prophetic years

There are a few other points of note concerning 42 months. When 42 is divided by God's number 7, the quotient is 6. 6 is one less than God, reinforcing that humanity can never be

God. 6 is considered the number of man. Adam was created on the 6th day. Likewise, 6 days were granted for labor and the 7th was commanded as rest and worship. As mentioned, 42 is closely associated with death, especially in judgment. The nation of Islam ruled over Jerusalem's abomination for 42 months, I Samuel 13 says King Saul ruled over Israel for 42 years; in another instance, 42,000 Ephraimites were killed-(Ephraim and Manasseh may have been the natural sons of Joseph but were adopted by Jacob); in another case, 42 relatives of King Ahaziah were killed. He was the 6th king of Judah and ruled for 2 years.

```
  6    Number of man
x 7    Perfection
 42    7 less than 49
```

Elisha's story addresses 42 who were mauled by 2 she-bears in II Kings 2. Elisha is depicted as sticking close to his teacher throughout Elijah's last day on earth in order to receive a special blessing. At the Jordan River Elijah's coat touches the water enabling both to cross over on dry land. 50 other disciples attempting to follow were cut off when the Jordan's flow quickly resumed. After Elisha receives his double portion of the Holy Spirit, Elijah ascends to heaven in a whirlwind depicted by horse-drawn chariots of fire, leaving behind only his coat. Then Elisha dawns the coat and parts the river in the same manner as Elijah had done. Shortly afterwards the 42 who mocked Elisha were mauled by 2 she-bears.

Several inferences can be made. Elisha's story parallels Moses' parting of the Red Sea, New Testament salvation, baptismal waters, deliverance, etc. But are we missing a more significant parallel? First, let us assess any correlation between the 2 she-bears and Israel. In Leviticus 26, God promises to disciple wayward Israelites 7 times with plagues from the beasts of the field. Perhaps, in Elisha's story, 42 people are just a microcosm of the unsaved portion from the Jewish nation. The bears are chosen because they symbolize plagues of war otherwise represented by Persia (and the Medes). The second bear is also a Persian invasion (which is also the 8th and like the 7th, Revelation 17) identified as the Sassanid Empire only to be followed by the Ottoman Turks. Sassanids and Turks are mostly New Testament Persian descendants. Second, it is interesting that an additional 50 disciples all knew Elijah would be "caught up" that very day in a whirlwind (or perhaps even a tornado) and could not follow after being "cut off" at the water's edge. Could this be a picture referencing a rapture? Are we supposed to know when Yeshua returns? Is it linked to a Sabbatical or Jubilee year? Could this be a specific warning to the Jewish lineage concerning salvation or being left behind? The Christian message has clearly permeated the Jewish culture enough to know the Gospel of Jesus Christ. Doesn't this message bear witness to the Feast of Sukkot? Finally, notice that after Elisha puts on Elijah's coat he carries on the prophetic role. Elisha has symbolically received the favor of God. This favor is a similar portrayal to Joseph's coat of many colors. Both seem to illustrate the saving grace of God. Perhaps this is a portrait of grace extending into the Messianic Age, or more specifically meant to imply the Messianic Jew. Notice the horse-drawn chariots of fire, a whirlwind, leaving behind clothes all seem to mimic a move by the Holy Spirit and a rapture-like second coming.

Notice the entry in 70 A.D. on the next chart. Herod's Temple was destroyed during the 8th Sabbatical year. The 8th Sabbatical is also the start of the 1st Sabbatical cycle. Could the temple's destruction in 70 A.D. be a foreshadowing of Revelation 11? Are the current mosques about to be destroyed? For decades terrorists have made various attempts to blow up both mosques constructed upon this temple mount. Israeli forces have prevented each attempt thus far. No doubt a successful rebel attack could provoke an unjustified armed outcry focused against Israel. The chart maps several significant dates worth examining. For example, could the 42nd Jubilee be indicating destruction on the horizon?

Sabbatical	Jubilee	Cycle	Event
14 AD	15 AD	7/7	2 Sabbaticals till Christ
28 AD		2/7	Christ ministry year 1
63 AD	64 AD	7/7	1 Jubilee after Christ
70 AD		*8th	2nd temple destroyed
504	505	7/7	10th Jubilee after Christ
994	995	7/7	20th Jubilee after Christ
1484	1485	7/7	30th Jubilee after Christ
1925	1926	7/7	40th Jubilee after Christ
1974	1975	7/7	41st Jubilee via Christ
1988		2/7	2 Sabbaticals added 14 AD
2023	2024	7/7	42nd Jubilee begins
2030		*8th	3rd temple destroyed
2037		2/7	2 Sabbaticals till end

Assuming that a similar temple destruction event occurs on the 8th Sabbatical cycle we can calculate the coming destruction as follows:

1974 A.D.	41st Jubilee from Christ begins
+ 49 years	1 Sabbatical cycle
2023 A.D.	42nd Jubilee from Christ begins
2023 A.D.	10/2/2024 The Last Jubilee
+ 7 years	1st Sabbatical also the 8th
2030 A.D.	Temple destruction

Is this the date that both mosques on the temple mount will be removed? Or is this a message of total desolation? Watch what happens when 40 Jubilees are added to the destruction date of Herod's temple in 70 A.D.

40	Jubilees
x 49	7 Sabbaticals
1960	years
1960 years	40 Jubilees
+ 70 A.D.	2nd Temple
2030 A.D.	Desolation

Does 40 represent a subcomponent of a Jubilee generation, for a time for testing? Are any events scheduled for 2030? Notice the outcome when 42 is applied to the presidential prophecy of 1988:

1988	Presidential prophecy
+42	Number of destruction
2030	8th Sabbatical of destruction

Could this be the unveiling entrance of a final Antichrist? Will this be packaged with a New One World Order? Will the One World Order be implemented via the United Nations? This coming chaos suggests another Tower of Bable-like event. Is it a coincidence that this computer age solves the language barrier? Even the software business is named Babble. Would this 2nd Tower of Bable event occur before or after a church rapture?

1997 A.D.	6000 expired years
+ 40 years	A time of testing
2037 A.D.	Great trouble

Is 2037 the end, or is 2030? Clearly, 2030-2037=7 years. It would be easy to suggest these are the final 7 vials of the Great Tribulation without more proof. Remember the outstanding question from the book series? What does the 49-year gap from 1988 through 2037 represent? That gap is no longer a mystery. Quite remarkably the dates tend to arrive at the same conclusion, 2037. Quite remarkable indeed.

1988 A.D.	Seer in the Way
+ 49 years	1 Sabbatical cycle
2037 A.D.	End of the Age

Despite the noise surrounding various dates, 2037 is uniquely linked to Christ's ministry. In addition, it is 49 years from 1988 and linked by a key 40-year Davidic reign over Jerusalem since Israel's founding in 1948. A 2nd 40-year reign may reflect Solomon's tenure till 2028. Should the 10 years of Moses be included, the final conclusive date arrives in 2038. This will be examined fully in due course.

1948 A.D.	Nationhood
+ 40 years	Davidic reign
1988 A.D.	Presidential prophecy

1988 A.D.	Presidential prophecy
+ 40 years	Solomon's reign
2028 A.D.	Possible rapture

2028 A.D.	Possible rapture
+ 10 years	Moses years
2038 A.D.	New Jerusalem

1988 is the 21st year from 1967 indicating a breakthrough year. It is also a Sabbatical year. These clues appear to be narrowing the window of probabilities. So, now let's press onward with the quest. What other relevant information might be found? More charts and data are still to come.

EIGHT IS ENOUGH

Some consider the Sabbath the first festival bringing the total number of major holidays to 8. However, there is another forgotten festival that begins on the 8th day. It commences after celebrating all 7 days of Sukkot. All the previous festivals point to this 8th day, particularly the last 3. As discussed, there are 7 annual events, 4 in the spring and 3 in the autumn. Overall, 3 celebrations are designed as feasts though the word festival is often substituted for any or all of these unique Jewish holidays:

Feast of Unleavened Bread	7-days
Feast of Weeks	(7x7) +1
Feast of Tabernacles	7-days

Each of these 3 feasts requires a pilgrimage to Jerusalem. Some were to remember past events, and some were meant to rehearse future events. All 7 festivals exist as a seasonally encoded message immune from calendar alterations. They illustrate an unmistakable 7,000-year cycle most of which is found in Leviticus 23. Mankind often focuses on the first 6,000 years because the last 1,000 years exist as a phase of rest, after civilization as we know it. The festivals serve as ageless mirrors and clues. They align with prophecies to defy Statistical probabilities. For example, Jesus was convicted on Nissan 10, the day of selection designated for the spotless lamb. 4 days later Jesus was crucified around 9 am on Nissan 14, Passover. Around 3 pm Jesus expired and was placed inside a tomb. That evening marks the Feast of Unleavened Bread, Nissan 15. Yeshua rose 3 days later (after Passover) on Nissan 18, Firstfruits. 3 days after Passover was also the 8th day (resurrection Sunday) after being selected as our scapegoat on Nissan 10. The Feast of Weeks starts the 7-week (49 days) count of Omer until Shavuot (Pentecost). Pentecost equates to a rebirth of the Spiritual portion of man. This spiritual revival was finished when a sinless man died on the cross. This goal could only be accomplished by an uncorrupted man. Since the only incorruptible being is God, the solution also had to be divine. After man's spiritual rebirth, only the restoration of the physical world around us remained unfinished. The takeaway should determine that Christ fulfilled all 4 festivals exactly as prescribed. It should go without saying, that the mathematical probabilities of these respective dates from thousand-year-old prophecies being completed by one person in this manner are astronomical. Yet the odds continue to increase when coupled with many other fulfilled prophecies. Here is a breakdown of events:

Event	Time	Date	Description
Nissan	30 AD	10th	Scapegoat selection
Passover	4 days	14th	Crucifixion 9 am
Unleavened Bread	1 day	15th	Removed after 3 pm Eve of 5th day
Firstfruits	3 days	18th	Resurrection 8th day
Weeks	49 days		Count of Omer
Shavuot	50 days		1st & 8th day/week

If we acknowledge the first 4 feasts as representing Yeshua's sacrifice for all sin, then the last 3-4 feasts might tell us about His 2nd coming. Rosh Hashanah, also known as Yom

Teruah, was already discussed as the day of shouting and falls on the 1st day of the 7th month of Tishri. The number 7 announces completion. The 7th seal declares the end of the Old Testament and the 7th trumpet announces the end of the elect's service on earth. This 7th trumpet might be the aha moment between lukewarm Christians and Jews. As previously stated, scripture calls for New Testament disciples to be caught up with the sound of the last trump. Would this correspond to the next U.S. presidential term?

Many Jews believe the following festival of Yom Kippur evokes that event rather than Yom Teruah. Herein contains a gap of 10 days from Yom Teruah and Yom Kippur. Which focus group has it right? Or could they both be correct? Ironically, most religious converts will miss the significance of Rosh Hashanah/Yom Teruah. The Jews look toward Yom Kippur to be reunited, and the average Christian remains ignorant of the timeliness of the event altogether. On average, only the Messianic Jew accepts the truth of each event. Much to my chagrin, this is likely due to popular seminary teaching and replacement theology. Replacement theology supplants the God-given Jewish positioning in exchange for the church, thereby diminishing the relevance of Judaism, the Hebrew culture, and the festivals. Yet God's commandments retain their value above the respect of man.

Extrapolating the supposition that the first rapture event on Tishri 1 (Yom Teruah) becomes obvious to some unbiased onlookers in that many believers will essentially vanish with no logical explanation, then it also may be reasonable to conclude that some might rethink their current religious perspective about the validity of Christianity. Specifically, if the Jew were to miss the first "catching away" at Yom Teruah, Yom Kippur could bring the missing ingredient of repentance enabling a 2nd chance to enter into the Kingdom of God. Whether Christ returns a 2nd time for payment during the Days of Awe or directly on Yom Kippur is not yet fully distinguishable. But if God has been covering Israel's sins since conception, maybe some will receive a second chance if obeying the commandments via observing each festival. Notice that in Revelation the High Priest begins the same process written in Leviticus that atones for sins. Also, in Revelation 7 we see what appears to be a 1st harvest of nations clothed in pure white apparel. Then a 2nd ingathering of nations is adorned in holy garments. This gives the impression of a 2nd opportunity, like Yom Kippur, to exercise faithful repentance. When defining Yom Ha-kippurim it literally means "day of coverings." One could make the case that Yahweh has been covering humanity's sins since He made the first animal sacrifice to clothe Adam and Eve in the Garden of Eden. From this vantage point, God can be perceived as taking a stance of Mercy and Grace. In fact, casting Adam and Eve from the garden was an act of mercy. Had either one eaten from the immortal tree after sinning, they would have been separated from God for eternity, trapped on the opponent's field forever.

But are there any other Old Testament signals given to eager observers? What signs can we ascertain to help define that last day? Books in the New Testament stress that the final days will be as in the days of Noah. So, let's see what that might entail. The word used to "cover" the pitch on Noah's Ark is the same reference used in the "Day of Atonement." Noah and his family were covered safely within the Ark while the earth was destroyed, washed, and cleansed. According to Yom Teruah, in the same way, those in Christ will be spared from destruction before the 2nd renewal. Eventually, this 2nd event represented by fire will culminate in the physical restoration of our body instigated by the actions that led to the cross. Jesus is the mirror of God leading to spiritual salvation. Likewise, Joshua is the mirror of Jesus in Exodus leading Israelites physically into the "Promise Land." It is no coincidence that they both carry the same name Yeshua. After the 7 days of Sukkot expire, the elect will enter the new Promise Land just as Joshua did at Jericho. The 8th day occurs after 40 years of wandering in the desert and living in tents. Sukkot mirrors the Ark "covering" by tabernacling with Christ. Pilgrims are a picture of the elect living in a temporary dwelling waiting for the earth to be reborn. Some think this may take another 1,000 years or more after the 2nd coming, Psalm 95. But Sukkot likely leads us to an 8th day, the unveiling of earth's finished restoration process. The book of Revelation calls that restoration place, "New Jerusalem." After observing this information laid out in chart form and applying a rather obscure 8th-day event called Shemini Atzeret the picture of God's intentions becomes more readily distinguishable. God intended this to be the Autumn Season of Remembrance.

Event	Length	Day	Description
Elul	40 days		Prayer until Yom Kippur
Yom Teruah	Unknown days 1-2	1st or 2nd	7th month - 7th trump 1st harvest "caught up"
Days of Awe	10 days		Judgment on earth Revelation 17 - 15 days
Yom Kippur	1 day	10th	Repented "ingathering" 2nd harvest
Sukkot	7 days	15th	Exposure to elements War and return
Shemini Atzeret	1 day	7000	1st & 8th day - 1,000 yrs. New Jerusalem

A finished portrait is plain to see once the 8th Day of Shemini Atzeret is added. The 8-day process mirrors the consecration of the priests in Leviticus 8-9. The significance parallels the 8th day of Noah and marries the 8th day of Jesus mentioned in the 4 spring festivals with the last 4 festivals in autumn. The feasts demonstrate death and a new beginning just as fall gives way to springtime. Yeshua ushers in new life and the Father heals creation. Leviticus 23 dictates this 8th day as a day of rest just as the Sabbath does and the extra day of Jubilee. This seems to be the day Jehovah dwells with mankind again, after the marriage and honeymoon. At his point marriage consummation has usurped the act of communion. Through our marriage in Christ, we are one with the Father. Remember, Christ redeemed our spirit on the 8th week of Pentecost; now, the Father will renew our bodies as He has fixed eternity in our hearts, Ecclesiastes 3. Thus, the number 8 represents a new beginning.

The 8th brings more significance when the reading of the Torah restarts in Genesis. According to the Messianic Sabbath Website, Simchat Torah always begins after the 8th day, Tishri 23. 8 days later in the next month of Cheshvan, rabbis launch the reading of creation and the flood. Cheshvan is the 8th month and means "separating destruction from life." Noah's Ark launched and rested 1 year later in the 8th month of Cheshvan. Does this suggest that the elect will enter New Jerusalem during the Hebrew 8th month? In Genesis, were Adam and Eve forced to leave the Garden of Eden during the 8th month? God was gracious enough to leave celebratory clues about the plan to restore all those who honor Him.

As established, the flood began in the 8th month of Cheshvan. Noah was 600 years old. When Noah reached age 601, he removed the Ark covering on Tishri 1. Does this imply that anyone not covered under the blood of the Lamb will not be "caught away" on Yom Teruah? Isn't this the mirror image of a lamb's Passover blood smeared above the doorposts of Old Testament believers? Or, does it mean that after the cleansing process, no more covering will be needed because everything will be restored? Perhaps the answer to both latter questions is yes. The 7th month of Tishri is an Akkadian word meaning "beginning." Among other things, it probably implies Yeshua returns at the New Beginning. Shemini Atzeret appears to be the beginning of New Jerusalem. It will likely not occur on an 8th Jubilee year, since the Jubilee year is 2024 and 2073. Or perhaps the new beginning brings attention to Sunday as the 8th day, thereby commanding devotion to the only Way...Christ Jesus? Is it possible that Shemini Atzeret will arrive on a Sunday? Indeed. Shemini Atzeret occurs on Sunday, October 12th-13th, 2036. The Jewish calendar registers the year as 2037.

At the writing of this book, the start of Jubilee 2024 has not yet come to pass. However, the midst of the 40th Sabbatical and Jubilee from Christ's ministry witnessed the rebirth of the nation of Israel in 1948 and the restoration of Jerusalem in 1967. Currently, the world resides within the 41st Jubilee until Tishri 2024-26 which introduces the potentially ominous number of 42. The 3rd year of the 42nd Sabbatical arrives at Rosh Hashanah 2027. Loosely interpreted, this parallels the 10th Jubilee prophesied by Rabbi Judah. My 1988 presidential prophecy extends 49 years in a similar Jubilee-like format pointing to a 2037 finale. This 2037 climax, was preceded by a 40-year mirror liken to Exodus. Just as the Israelites wandered until delivered into the Promised Land, so will this be a time of testing from 1997-2037.

    1997 6,000 years
    + 40 Testing period
    2037 End of Age

As proven, the actual Jubilee cycle is acknowledged in the 50th year as pictured in the 2024-2025 Sabbatical year. Remember, the 8th Sabbatical week is also the 1st week of the next cycle. This perpetual cycle displays an all-encompassing perspective as found in Psalm 90:2 and Nehemiah 9:5. This adds depth to Isaiah 44:6-8, and Revelation 22:13. Discovery of the correct Jubilee year has not yet successfully filtered into the Jewish and Christian cultures. The current Jewish calendar states the next Shmita year is 9/20/28-9/09/29 although they openly profess not knowing the Jubilee year. Of course, this is a huge problem since without a Jubilee as the anchor date there can be no confirmed 7th Shmita year. Applying anything other than the yearly Sabbatical is simply a guesstimate. But now that we know the Jubilee year is 2024, we can determine 2023 as a Shmita Sabbatical. That also defines 2024-2025 as the 8th Sabbatical year. Sequencing years by increments of 7 we can deduce future Shmita Sabbatical dates as 2030 and 2037 which are also logged within the parameters of a 42nd Jubilee cycle. If the number 42 is truly a meaningful hint within the Jubilee cycle it must be logged onto the diagram for consideration.

Based upon learning Yeshua's 1st year of ministry was initiated during the Passover and Festival of Unleavened Bread in 28 A.D., we can subtract these years from the previous Sabbatical/Jubilee of 14 A.D. This context instructs us to consider adding 14 years (or 2 Shmitas) to the 2023 Sabbatical/Jubilee date. That would permit us to chart Yeshua's subsequent return on Shemini Atzeret, 2037. But this may not include any rapture-type events. Albeit this is the same date regarded as 1 generation of 70 years from 1967 A.D., further suggesting a narrow window of impending doom. Determining the exact moment of a pre-rapture event may prove to be more elusive. Several Rosh Hashanah dates are selected with various benchmarks endorsing these as the highest probability. One caveat to remember, any Shmita Sabbatical or Jubilee can claim 1 additional year not listed on the chart. In any event, the information suggests a high probability of Yeshua's call summoning for His elect will take place within the next 7 years. The dominant question becomes which Rosh Hashanah is it? Which year is the most meaningful to God? Which day holds the key that unlocks the secret of His return? Contrary to popular belief, the day and year certainly won't be arbitrary. Follow along as the window narrows again.

The Last Jubilee:

Sabbatical	Jubilee	Year	Event
		1948	Israel nation
1967			Jerusalem reunified
1974	1975	1976	40th Jubilee from Christ
1988	1988 + 49 2037	8th son of Jesse	David 40 years + 1948 41st Jubilee from Christ The Last Jubilee begins*
2023	2024	2025	41st Jubilee from Christ 70th Jubilee from Exodus
28 AD		2026	42nd Jubilee cycle begins Ends on Sunday 9/11 3 years till cross Extra Jubilee year

2028		2029		Unsubstantiated Shmita 1988+40 years Solomon
2029		2030*		8th day-Sunday 9/9-11 42nd Jubilee from Christ 6th year of a Sabbatical Shmita release 2030*
Sep-Oct 2036- 2037	1997 +40 & 1967 +70 End		2038	2 Shmita's from 14 AD 8th year of a Sabbatical 42nd Jubilee from Christ Shmita release *Last Jubilee from 1988 1 generation from 1967
2072	2073		2074	42nd Jubilee ends 10th Rabbi Judah 2067+7

Noting the calendar issues, an adjustment may be possible for some dates, plus or minus a year. The goal is to be close, not exact. If precise happens, all the better. After all, the entire religion of Judaism celebrates the incorrect Shmita year, Sabbatical cycle, and Jubilee years. Notwithstanding, unless another clue presents itself the current window of opportunity has been radically reduced. Accordingly, it might be wise to begin prayer preparation in each upcoming Elul and reverently evaluate our spiritual standing. Remember Elul begins the month before Rosh Hashanah and extends 30 days into the 1st day of Tishri. Elul continues through Rosh Hashanah until Yom Kippur (10 days later) completing 40 days of prayer. Could Elul somehow be participating in this autumn message in a deeper, more powerful way? Breaking down the calendar design the first 30 days are followed by the last 10 days through the Days of Awe. Using scriptural consistency, each day can be converted into years. The next scenario displays the same date already established to end the age.

1997 A.D.	6000 expired years
+ 40 years	Exodus time of testing
2037 A.D.	End

1997 A.D.	6000 expired years
+ 30 years	Yom Teruah/Rosh Hashanah
2027 A.D.	Approximate harvest

1997 A.D.	6000 expired years
+ 10 years	Days of Awe/Yom Kippur
2037 A.D.	End

Observing the overall theme of 40 years recognizes a reward for those who pass the test. Noah passed the test of rain for 40 days and 40 nights. Although, Moses failed his test in Kadesh during the 40th year. The background of the story describes the area as having no water. Having no water in the land is a written depiction of the lack of living water, meaning ungodly people lived there. Several instances in scripture involve drought in connection with ungodliness. Kadesh is thought to be the area south of Israel and probably one area some of the descendants of Ishmael settled. At that time the Hebrew people were displeased, and Moses angrily struck the rock to bring forth much-needed water, Numbers 20. Previously the 40-year water supply via prophetess Miriam's well had dried up since her death. In the totality of these facts, it can be deduced that by Mose striking the rock instead of speaking the Word of God as commanded, he mirrored the future rejection of the Jews toward the coming Messiah as pictured in Psalm 18 and Matthew 7. For this reason, Moses could not enter the Promised Land. Today the Jew lives in the land but still largely does not recognize Jesus as the Living Water, the Word of God, or Emmanuel-God with us.

As displayed in the calculations an imposed time limit exists, apparently ending around 2037. The first hurdle arrives halfway between 2023-2030. This previously determined Shmita Sabbatical is bisected at Yom Teruah 2026-2027. For those observing Adonai and Elohim respectively 2026-2027 might represent the 1st harvest followed by a 2nd chance after Yom Kippur repentance. Since this festival is uniquely a Jewish ritual, the date could specify a 2nd chance harvest for Israel after 2027. Obviously, those observing Adonai and Elohim earlier might fall under different parameters or feasts and therefore demand different symbolism. It is not God's character to leave us ignorant. At a minimum, He promised to tell us the season, which we now know.

Interestingly, Rosh Hashanah/Yom Teruah is widely accepted by Messianic Jews as the last trump. Historically, Yom Kipper is recognized as having similar representation. Rosh Hashanah begins on the 1st day of the 7th month and Yom Kippur is celebrated on the 15th, trailing 14 days later. Assuming this is not another accident, we know there are 3 sets of 14 generations to Christ. Could this be signaling the 4th and final set at the end? Could this be a reflection to remind us there are 14 years from the Jubilee of 14 AD until the start of Christ's ministry in 28 AD? Could that 14-day gap also be the atoning difference between a 1st and 2nd rapture? Or is it the time from the Last Jubilee until the end? Atone means AT-ONE. No doubt the marriage makes us whole. That idea is incorporated within most wedding vows today. Will we all become one after Yom Kippur?

The 2030-2037 Sabbatical seems almost irrelevant unless you are left behind on earth after others are caught up with Christ. But what if the rapture doesn't look like what the church presupposes it to be? In either event, will you be inquisitive enough to care or will chaos rule your day? You may ponder these specifics and more should they be deemed significant. For our purposes, the last 7 years must attest to the marriage and honeymoon to the Lamb of God. The elect must be prepared for the groom, though already in heaven. This is prior to preparation for Shemini Atzeret 2036-2038. Today, only the restoration of the physical world around us remains incomplete. That may sound motivating to some but downright scary to others.

SAVING THE WORLD

"We the Heads of State and Government and High Representatives, meeting at the United Nations Headquarters in New York from 25-27 September 2015 as the Organization celebrates its 70th anniversary, have decided today on new global Sustainable Development Goals. At the heart of this plan are the 17 Sustainable Development Goals (ADGs). From ending poverty to reducing hunger, from improving access to education and healthcare to fighting against inequalities, the SDGs are "an urgent call for action by all countries – developed and developing – in a global partnership," said the UN.

The United Nations website goes on to say, "We resolve, between now and 2030, to end poverty and hunger everywhere; to combat inequalities within and among countries to build peaceful, just, and inclusive societies; to protect human rights and promote gender equality and the empowerment of women and girls and to ensure the lasting protection of the planet and its natural resources. We resolve also to create conditions for sustainable, inclusive, and sustained economic growth, shared prosperity, and decent work for all, considering different levels of national development and capacities."

There is a lot to unpack when explaining the complexities of the United Nations. However, the date 2030 in the previous paragraph should catch our eye immediately. It is time to investigate if there is a correlation between events related to the end times and the agenda of this organization. At first glance, the intentions expressed by the U.N. appear to be genuinely good-hearted. However, the subtle undertones have teeth. After all, such a far-reaching organization must have supreme authority in order to achieve such lofty goals. The sole goal of ending poverty is fundamentally impossible even if total economic control is obtained by only one entity. Scripture tells us that the poor will always be with us. Even still, the whole world continues under the persistent illusion that this organization can solve this realm's problems if all nations would only bequeath their authority. This construct is not attainable. However, poverty can be subjectively achieved through a redefinition of the term, which socialism permits. Such a version of humanitarianism can then be applied as a successful measure of achievement. And, therein begins the rub. Our failure as a society doesn't mean we shouldn't attempt to feed the poor, and it certainly should not imply that we will forever end all poverty everywhere. Then where does the disconnect rest?

First, we must trust the scripture found in Matthew 26:11. This achievement of eliminating all poverty can only be obtained by changing the human condition of the heart. Humans are what they are and when they are freely supplied with necessities, they tend to cease personal improvement. Societies have proven man's inherent nature of laziness over centuries of existence. The nineteen hundreds didn't require Marx to explain labor, it needed Marx to exploit ignorance and start the final communist movement. So, it is not so much the goal of feeding the hungry that is amiss, for that is the carrot, it is the disingenuous goal of gaining total control. The objective is always to change course toward the real agenda that is evil. Denying the problem of true spirituality will not make this problem go away. It will be their ruin.

Believe it or not, not everyone wants to achieve the same goals in life. Some work harder than others. Some people work for the finer things in life. Some are blessed by the hand of God with prosperity, and some are not for whatever reason. Marxism superimposes a devious work ethic with the idea that the lower class is suppressed into a lifestyle thrust upon them. Over time, Marxism becomes the driving force behind jobs, business, and total control. All socialism leads to communism. We call it "centralized" control. Marx designed it that way. The virus starts slowly, eventually penetrating all facets of government until a total shutdown is needed to purge the system. Lenin, Hitler, Mao, and Mussolini were there to redirect those pieces and capture all control. They became responsible for everyone's prosperity. We call it totalitarianism. That redistribution of wealth presents itself in all forms, including all natural resources which is often coined "environmentalism." This philosophy is not new. My previous book rightly researches this term in a 2000-year-old ideology known as Zoroastrianism. Unbeknownst to most ascribing to preserving Mother Nature, a select few have highjacked this idea of preservation to control world finances. Marxism permits the coercive framework for subverting funds from various altruistic endeavors. It chooses winners and losers on the premise of working together to save the planet. Its true nature seeks to manipulate every nation through trade laws, punishments, and monetary transactions. This will eventually derail world peace and the preservation they claim to promote. It steals whatever it desires from people's pockets. It is divisive. And, a house divided amongst itself will never stand.

Socialism simulates a better form of equality by exchanging it for equity. In that form of rule, the government decides what is equal by an ever-changing sliding slide rule. That type of oppression redefines societal norms indiscriminately and applies arbitrary pressure judicially. Consequently, this ideology seeks no less than total control over every corner of existence under the pretext of saving the world from the ignorant citizens among them. Such a Machiavellian methodology cannot be underscored. Marxism is the final plague that afflicts the last societies on earth. It is the lake where Satan soon resides, "cut off" from the river of life. Until then, Lucifer attempts to "cut off" mankind from freedom and inalienable rights. These are not the same rights proposed in the first paragraph of the United Nations website. Inalienable rights mark equality under God. They are unremovable as life, liberty, and the pursuit of happiness. John Locke suggested property rights in lieu of happiness. This is paramount in a free enterprise system. For this reason, Socialists persecute the middle class. Human Rights and equity are norms substituted by atheistic authorities.

Now, it should become clear that while socialism professes cooperation between government and citizens, it can only lead to oppression. In truth, there is no end game where authoritarianism does not continually encroach upon the freedoms of individuals, just as Marx confessed. He said all roads lead to the same style of oppression, communism. In modern-day discussions, society pretends this repression is only represented within communism. Though, Marx was clear by implicating socialism as the origin. That was the nature of his design. This type of control is articulated on the U.N. website but covertly omits these buzzwords. We read forceful 2030 decisions contractually cemented mostly by unelected representatives "to take bold and transformative steps... we pledge that no one will be left behind... We are determined to foster peaceful, just, and inclusive societies which are free from fear and violence. There can be no sustainable development without peace, and no peace without sustainable development." Thus, the United Nations' connection with developing nations was purposely and economically intertwined with forceful intentions but promoted as peaceful.

The second book in this series identifies this era by mirroring Revelation's Little Season. Therein, we see the baton handed from the Ottoman Empire, after their defeat, to Germany. This new information indicates that the baton has been passed once again; this time to the United Nations after Germany's defeat in 1945. Interestingly, the first attempt at unification in the 20th century was unsuccessful. Woodrow Wilson began that first effort under the League of Nations in 1920. He was the first Progressive president in the U.S.

Today, progressives permeate both the Democrat and Republican parties. Many citizens are unaware that progressivism is a code word for socialism. To make matters worse, many worldwide have been conditioned to accept this ideology in exchange for freedom. They are taught its promises of false security when exchanged for liberty. In any event, the League of Nations collapsed under the weight of the Great Depression. The socialist baton continued its forceful rise in Germany. Here we see that Hitler was an Antichrist of this last century until his defeat in 1944. For this reason, the League of Nations could not proceed in the next evolutionary handoff until WWII ended. Again, it would not be until after Germany failed that full authorization could transition to the United Nations. In this way, the United Nations has likened itself to the New Holy Roman Empire. Though some involved with the United Nations may have good intentions, true motives can rarely be perceived from a human perspective, if at all. Intentions come from the heart and the battleground competes in a spiritual realm. To win this battle we must engage the enemy. To engage the opposition successfully, we must identify spiritual reality and be subjects on the winning side. This requires prayer. Any governmental authority that plans to be successful outside of prayerful commitment to the one true sovereign God will fail. No empire, no matter how well intended, powerful, or unified will achieve lasting peace without acknowledging the Peacemaker.

Notice the contradiction of statements in this next U.N. quote: "We reaffirm that every State has, and shall freely exercise, full permanent sovereignty over all its wealth, natural resources, and economic activity. We will implement the Agenda for the full benefit of all, for today's generation and for future generations. In doing so, we reaffirm our commitment to international law and emphasize that the Agenda is to be implemented in a manner that is consistent with the rights and obligations of states, under international law." Close inspection shows that state laws are subject to the obligations of this international agreement. Historically, this ultimately is the case when treaties are signed. This is one glaring reason why war is often the unintended consequence. The second reason for conflict should be more conspicuous to onlookers. Keep in mind, this contract was never agreed to by the citizenry of participating nations. Thus, it seeks to supersede the people's will. And, even if peace is temporarily achieved, a forced peace is never a lasting peace. So, once again, while on its face such an organization professes goodwill, the devil always seems to be hidden within the details.

What might be other details hidden covertly within this profession of peace? Woven into their ideology under equal rights is the implementation of a liberal interpretation toward gender perspective ensuring universal sexual and reproductive rights. This is backed by taxpayer's dollars disguised as healthcare services, family planning, and education. All these services are to be extended to migrants who seem to possess all the same rights as national citizens, thereby creating a world citizen category. To accelerate each category's foothold an orderly and regular international migratory relocation will be implemented until the transitional goals are cemented. At some point, tourism movements will be limited under the guise of sustainable resources. These limitations will be implemented with the assistance of naive business partners and affluent individuals. This statement depicts these clear objectives: "We commit to making fundamental changes in the way that our societies produce and consume goods and services. Governments, international organizations, the business sector, and other non-state actors and individuals must contribute to changing unsustainable consumption and production patterns, including through the mobilization, from all sources, of financial and technical assistance to strengthen developing countries' scientific, technological, and innovative capacities to move towards more sustainable patterns of consumption and production." Plainly expressed, governments will begin choosing winners in businesses based upon their willingness to assist in the 2030 deadline. Those businesses and individuals who do not conform will be crushed under the full weight of regulation, litigation, and economic retribution. In theory, this must occur in order to force all unwilling subjects into submission before the 2030 deadline. But why 2030? Are there other implications below the surface? If these implications are hidden, they must be important enough to shine the light on them.

Using the previous book information something interesting emerges. First, the United Nations was adopted in 1945, and the climate agenda began implementation in 2015. This computation shows the space of 70 years. This is the length of a Psalm generation. Is this confirmation that the opposition hijacked this political organization?

    2015 United Nations climate agreement
    -1945 United Nations founded
    70 years or 1 generation

    2030 U.N. Climate maturity date
    -2015 Persian Zoroastrian agreement
    15 yrs. 2 hours prophetic time=15 days

Examining the second calculation above the question arises if this 15-year maturity date might simulate the same 2 hours in Biblical prophecy as calculated in both previous books. It might be a stretch to assume this although this could be considered the antichrist hours just as the antichrist also uses months. This might be a contextual departure to convert hours to days, and then to years, so more verification needs to substantiate this theory. But it is worth mentioning because the Antichrist measures in different time symbolism such as months instead of days. So, hours could be a similar ungodly deviation from Godly days to years.

Recognizing the 2030 date as the 8th Sabbatical week we can perceive that the U.N. climate control agreement will begin to dissolve in economic and political failure causing massive destruction. Based on historical events such as the demolition of the second temple in 69-70 A.D., which falls on an 8th Sabbatical cycle, we can reasonably conclude that 2029-2031 will be an exceptionally dreadful phase, even if only for Jerusalem. During this 8th Sabbatical, both temples were destroyed approximately 33 days before Rosh Hashanah. Interestingly, the flag of Israel carries the star of David which numerically represents 33. As for the United States, we can only pray that the mounting antisemitism quells. Hopefully, this country will support the peace of Jerusalem and will not be included in the final rising opposition to the Holy City. And, by peace, I do not mean to propose peace at all costs.

Notwithstanding, it must be said that while many are sympathetic to the environment there is no proven model submitted for scientific study supporting climate change. However, some theories have been presented, and various scientists have signed petitions supporting climate change theory. To my knowledge, only one scientific model was ever submitted for analysis. That model was proven to contain outliers. Thus, in the absence of science, the goal is to invoke social pressures through activism as seen in this next quote. "We the peoples who are embarking today on the road to 2030...will involve governments as well as parliaments, the UN system and other international institutions, local authorities, indigenous peoples, civil society, business and the private sector... the scientific and academic community." In the absence of proof, we see hyperbole. During this absence of facts, the focus shifted from an Ice Age to Global Warming to Climate Change, all within 50 years. Ironically, the very movement claiming to save the planet will become the nail in the coffin. The model requiring closer study is the effect of nuclear power at the atomic level as it relates to atmospheric deterioration. Although, the prospect of such a study being published will likely never transpire as it does not support their end-game intentions. This mimics Einstein's original worry before the first atomic bomb detonation. His concern was the chain reaction of events as it related to the melting of subatomic elements which essentially presents the same concern as nuclear power. Widespread, long-term usage of this power source will degrade the atmosphere. Besides, recent scientific studies have pointed to unlimited energy sources at the subatomic level. That is the key to future free energy. How long that might take to harness is the question.

At present, the name for this 2030 end-game event is called "The Great Reset." This new law of the land clearly says, "States are strongly urged to refrain from promulgating and applying any unilateral economic, financial or trade measures not in accordance with international law and the Charter of the United Nations that impede the full achievement of economic and social development, particularly in developing countries...We recognize the need to assist developing countries in attaining long-term debt financing, debt relief, debt restructuring, and sound debt management as appropriate." Much of this is achieved through the International Monetary Fund or the World Bank Group which is chiefly aided by United States tax dollars without consent of the governed. Sadly, once a nation is on the hook for debt financing, it can be more easily coerced into following the protocols of this new agenda. Although, recently there has been some push-back among second-tier countries. Perhaps some that push back have discovered that lending money to your adversaries may also fund wars against freedom-loving countries. A few countries have begun to seek more self-reliant agendas.

Lately, oil-rich nations have been rallying together to recruit opposition against the current monetary payment system, SWIFT. They are attempting to procure an alternative electronic method of transferring funds that could threaten to dethrone the U.S. dollar as the world currency. This would lead to worldwide economic disaster, particularly within the United States. The primary catalyst prompting some departures was the freezing of sovereign Russian assets after the invasion of Ukraine (Crimea). Bold economic sanctions are typically viewed by history as a primary catalyst to war which normally designates the final ingredient for war. This constitutes a ready-made fuse for 2030 that only needs a spark. Currently, sanctions have forced Russia to employ a costly shadow fleet of oil tankers brokered by Dubai as indiscrete middlemen. Once a ship leaves Russian waters the oil is transferred to another spoofed ship. The second spoofed tanker transfers the delivery of the prohibited black gold. So, in reality, the objective to eliminate the possibility of buying or selling is not yet obtainable. Cryptocurrency could be that final digital asset that controls all trade and payments if things don't fall apart sooner rather than later. Regardless, when it comes to a nation requiring high demand for a commodity such as oil, their economic needs will outweigh moral attributes if such a thing exists. All subversive actions launched as an end run on these United Nations legislative sanctions should also be a clear indictment of any clean fuel premise. The current technology will not support the notion of surviving without natural resources like oil no matter how noble the idea or how many mouthpieces spout otherwise. The purchase of Iran's sanctioned oil bears this out. Both countries are using Bitcoin instead of U.S. dollars. Perhaps the U.S. and the U.N. will decide to void the use of Bitcoin altogether and tighten financial sanctions. Undoubtedly, these decisions will produce a chain reaction leading to other unintended consequences; the race for nuclear power taking center stage. Of course, the eventual outcome of these actions will cause spillover effects resulting in World War III. Until then, expect intentional shortages, consequential rationing such as food and health care, and the systematic undermining of the rule of law.

These officials may also decide to curb the world's demand for resources through animal and population control, whether directly or indirectly. Sports will be promoted as the world's panacea just as the Colosseum symbolized Roman culture centuries ago. And, before that let us not forget the Tower of Babel. The Tower of Bable represents what mankind refuses to remember. This Babylonian temple signifies the pride and arrogance of humanity who repetitively attempt to equate themselves with God by eliminating Him from the solution. Just as in the days of Noah, man thinks he can save himself. Professing Christians are no less guilty of this act of idolatry. This is highly evident by the popular idea that acknowledging God is equivalent to pursuing Him. Fooling ourselves into thinking that having a belief in God equates to a personal relationship with the Creator is the height of self-deception. In this instance, those who believe are no better off than the atheists running the asylum. Even demons believe... James 2:19. The root of the problem facing society is the lack of daily soaking prayer. This absence of prayer demonstrates active avoidance. It shows no desire or need for a relationship that involves God with day-to-day decisions. Likewise, a world-ruling system that avoids reliance on the one who is the only answer exhibits the personification of pride. As evidenced throughout history, arrogance comes before every fall. Modern-day conflicts often seek to assert prideful control over one's life through our feelings. Feelings can never effectively rule over individuals. In reality, all personal and governmental controls should be handed over to the only spiritual King with the ability, power, grace, and mercy to apply all those freedoms and laws. Only a change of heart recognizes these principles and produces enough wisdom necessary to correct the collision course headed our way, if at all possible.

In light of this, the people selected to run governments make a difference. One key governmental officeholder is Antonio Guterres. Antonio Guterres is the 9th Secretary-General of the United Nations. His past exhibits a long history of activity involving the Socialist International, a worldwide organization of social democratic political parties. Sidebar: anytime the words social democratic are slammed together it should raise a red flag. Commingling words like social and democratic are more of an oxymoron meant to cajole lazy listeners. As explained, the two ideologies are incompatible. Even more disturbing, Antonio Guterres has expressed deep sympathy for the terrorist organization called Hamas. The secretary-general is the United Nations Chief Administrative Officer elected to 5-year terms. All nine secretary-generals up to this point have served 2 terms. This position is also the head of the Secretariat which is 1 of 6 principle organs of the United Nations. The main headquarters is located on 42nd Street in New York City. To the astute reader, these numbers might bring pause. The wisest reader asks the question who will become the 10th Secretary-General?

Retracing the history of the United Nations climate agenda legislation means the world is halfway through the 15-year "environmental" agreement. At the time of this book, there are less than 6 years left until the 2030 deadline to accomplish its goals. A huge hindrance to maintaining United Nations peace started in 2023. With 7 years left on the docket, Hamas broke the peace against Israel 1 day after the 50th year considered to be the first Yom Kippur War in 1973. Quite prophetically, the latest October attack fell on Shemini Atzeret. After reviewing other post-1967 altercations the 1972 Munich Massacre on Rosh Hashanah stood out. It was the last puzzle piece linking current events with the fall feasts. A macro view shows that all the fall festivals have been covered in blood. Remarkably, blood has been spilled in the order of each festival and every feast has been covered. In Genesis 6 Noah refers to Hamas as violence. When we see smoke, we assume there is fire. Where there is violence, there will be bloodshed. October 7th, 2023, should be called the Shemini Atzeret War. Armageddon might be the only blood left to shed. And, the only celebration remaining lies outside the boundaries of Israel.

Many will eventually migrate into asking one underlying question, "Will the church generally support the ideology behind the impending 2030 reset?" Surely not the enlightened church core. Yet, many inside the church today are quite comfortable giving in to the constant barrage of socialistic propaganda. Yet, is it incorrect to conclude that socialism is incompatible with individual freedoms such as worship? Marx answered that all authoritarian governments eventually expand to the point of total control. Consequently, this control seeks to infringe upon the right to worship freely. As this disease begins slowly, it is the subtlety of socialism that masks its true intentions. Once again, the confusion centers around the removal of equality with the substitution for equity. Though it gains power by promising wealth, the context of equality only exists on paper. In reality, all lower subjects are equally poor and powerless to alter their circumstances as the state assumes the role of who gets what and how much. Thus, the state locks in everyone's fate for limited self-achievement. Socialism deceitfully rises to power through the ignorant and unsuspecting as it aims to pit the larger working class against the wealthy. It is the feel-good religion for the godless, pretending to be what it is not. This religion seeks to absolve its citizens of duty by promoting victims which sets the final snare. Since everyone is positioned as a victim, forgiveness evaporates. Forgiveness is not an attribute of self-righteousness. Morality is traded for litigiousness and the system breaks down under the weight of corruption. Everyone in the game competes for whatever they can get out of it. Thus, the system becomes the scapegoat of immorality and must be replaced. For example, systemic racism inside the government can only be excommunicated by destroying the authorities in power. Yet, the people are the system. Therefore, the people condemn themselves. The replacement system will be as corrupt as the people who devise it. By all accounts, the die has been cast. The people of Babylon have handed over their freedoms under the guise of saving the planet only to destroy it. The handwriting is on the wall, Daniel 5.

THE U.S. IN HEBREW HISTORY

Now that the background information on the United Nations has been adequately addressed it is understandable why some feel the United States bears responsibility for creating this international entity. It has identifiably altered its course in the last 10 years. But make no mistake, this organization is not liable for all mankind. People run governments. People are responsible for governments, and people are responsible for themselves. The most effective thing we can do is pray, and the least we should do is pray. An unproductive attitude produces a scapegoat mentality in an attempt to absolve our complicit nature. Let us not become the victim via our own deceptive hands.

In Revelation, there is a scene of the High Priest cleansing the temple and offering sacrifices. This directly correlates to the Festival of Yom Kippur. The 3rd sacrifice on Yom Kippur consists of 2 goats. The goats are mirror opposites of good and evil. One goat is offered to cleanse the sanctuary and the other is loosed into the wilderness of Azazel, never to return, Leviticus 16. The 2nd goat carries the blame for sins from the people and a ram is burned for the whole nation. Paralleling the 1st goat's purpose of becoming a sacrifice of atonement the 2nd goat represents the leader who rebelled against God but is not forgiven. Azazel stands for a host of false gods including the Bull god, Satan, etc. Many of those names are listed in Seer in the Way. The wilderness would logically symbolize outer darkness and violence void of any peace or nature of God's goodness. This Day of Atonement or at-one-ness primarily suggests cleansing of the mercy seat. The altar must be performed before Jesus returns. Once again, this relates to wandering in the desert for 40 years, cleansing ourselves from sin to live in the presence of God lest we be cast out unworthy or unpurified. For disciples, they are worthy through Christ's blood from the cross. They are exempt from Azazel. This is the final purification process. For the unpurified, it suggests that intentional crimes do irreversible damage even corrupting the whole world such that it must be burned up as a sacrificial offering. Hebrews 9 and Revelation 1 clearly explain this reasoning through fellowship with Adoni. Marriage to the Master completes our at-one-ness to Elohim. For this reason, those observing Adonai and Elohim respectively represent the 1st harvest. Those exhibiting feasts through the Father and the Son might later be offered a 2nd chance after repentance as expressed during Yom Kippur. Until our sins are put down forever, we have a 5-fold ministry. Upon passing over, those gifts shall be burned. Until that Jubilee, we are supposed to be unified through the Holy Spirit as apostles, prophets, evangelists, pastors, and teachers as listed in Hebrews 10. New Jerusalem will offer a new man, a new Adam. All along God has been intentionally restoring all things until that day of New Jerusalem. Until then prayer is our access to His Spirit and power. Yeshua is our 1st, last, and permanent sacrifice.

In 1997, Ishmael entered the political scene at the start of the 40 years of testing. Later, he proclaimed that the United States should receive the 2nd goat bound to Azazel by professing allegiance to the opposition. This marks the moral and financial decline of the United States. Historically, the United States is a snapshot of Moses. Moses' life is divided into 3 sets of 40 years. In the first phase, he lived protected by Pharaoh. In the second phase, Moses was a shepherd in the wilderness. The last 40 years was spent leading the Israelites out of Egypt. Likewise, the United States will have 3 equal sets of time. It begins under the protection of protestant England, then the small country shepherds its' way into spiritual adulthood and branches off. Finally, the country protects Israel into nationhood just as a big brother is expected to do. Another perspective can be viewed from

1917 through 2037. In the first 40 years, the United States became a world power after WW I in 1917; then the space race and nuclear power became firsts; finally, the United States would continue to assist Israel militarily for the next 40 years until 2037 or ruin, Numbers 13:25 and 14:34.

The relationship between Israel and the United States often confounds people and visibly irritates antisemites. Yet, when asked many don't truly have reasonable responses why they are antisemitic or why they hate the U.S. for protecting Israel. They simply are driven by their wants and by their environment. They trap themselves into group thinking. But beyond doubt, the greatest divide falls between religious dogma. Many such groups dominating the news originated in the Middle East. Some say the Jewish and Arab divide originates with Ishmael and Isaac. Regardless of the starting point, the anger was deeply rooted numerous generations ago. Historically, Ishmael became the fatherless outcast, and Isaac is honored in place of the 1st born from Abraham and Hagar. Unknowingly, Ishmaelites widely denounce their original Father to this day. Jews and Arabs have been fighting ever since and will continue to do so unless repentance is sought via the blood of Christ. This forgiveness must be applied within their lives individually for the conflict to conclude. Yet, there is a cry in Revelation 18 for Ishmael to come out of her, meaning the false religion consuming the region. This has largely been overlooked or applied to the unsaved as a whole. But the context clearly addresses a more specific clientele designated especially for these last days. All specific participants who wish to forgo terrorizing neighbors should heed that call and return to the God of Abraham, David, and Yeshua.

The establishment of Israel as a nation is often blamed for most of the conflict today, especially regarding Palestine. Without splintering into various arguments, the point for our purposes is that the United Nations decided to reestablish Israel in 1948 under minimal guidelines. 3 nations, France, England, and the United States spearheaded that cause. As the United States repositioned itself into a dominant world power it assumed the role of a big brother to Israel. To date, the United States is the lone superpower to stand with Israel and against the latest U.N. resolutions condemning the tiny nation. However, the relationship of the United States and Israel might resemble that brotherly role much more deeply than many ever anticipated. That relationship may be better expressed to resemble the tribe of Ephraim or Manasseh. At one point, both tribes replaced Dan as the 12th tribe.

While it is possible to derive parallels between these 2 Hebrew tribes expressed with the likeness of England and the United States for most it is more palatable to promote Genesis 48 for this endeavor. Genesis 48 invokes the usage of the fish as a prophetic Christian symbol thousands of years before a Messiah. This is more acceptable for those who prefer not to acknowledge a possible remnant of Jewish DNA. For our purposes, there are no claims herein to prop up any particular ethnic group over another. But Hosea 7 mentions that Ephraim has mixed seed(s). America is known as the melting pot of the world. She symbolizes freedom of worship which is sponsored by strength in Christianity. Is it possible that Jesus communicated this reality even as He fed the 5 (grace) thousand in Luke 9? Could the 5 loaves represent the Word and law as written by Moses in the 5 books of the Torah? Are the 2 fish linking Genesis with the 2 houses of Israel? Afterwards, the leftovers consisted of 12 baskets of broken pieces. This can easily be a picture of the 12 tribes scattered across many waters only to be unveiled on the last day.

Now that we can get a sense of the role the United States has played through divine intervention and the modern-day political environment what is left? The final era is thought to be predicated upon a new type of financial system. Congress eventually adopted this new banking system in 1913 known as the Federal Reserve. Today, every major country uses the Federal Reserve banking payment processing system. Consequently, the U.S. dollar became the world currency and presently maintains that dominant position. So, with all this power over the world economics who owns the Fed? Technically, the Fed is privately owned by banks. It is overseen by appointees and to a lesser extent by elected officials. The main objective of the Fed is to control inflation and unemployment. Thus, the Fed is closely tied to the World Bank in that they both profess to guide global economic stability through lending policies. The World Bank Group is technically part of the United Nations and collectively owned by member countries. But only the Fed controls interest rates. And, since the dollar remains the world's reserve currency, any action the Fed takes to raise or lower the cost of lending reverberates globally.

The core question for economies today, is what causes the Fed to raise or lower interest rates? The long answer offered in economic circles reflects the political leaning of the establishment. For example, when economies get overheated the Fed's job is to raise interest rates in order to slow down purchases. Slowing purchases reduces inflation but increases unemployment. So, the job requires delicate maneuvering particularly when increasing or decreasing the money supply. Too much money in supply or liquidity can also be inflationary. But, the number one issue agitating inflationary pressures today seeks to undermine the entire banking system. That instigator unequivocally resides as debt. This takes the form of personal and national debt. Because governments have taken the political position of socialism for various reasons, they are inclined to tack on debt like never before for several reasons. At higher levels, debt becomes inflationary and unmanageable because too much cash is needed to pay interest. At current levels, the ability to service the debt is quickly becoming unsustainable. So, unless the citizenry insists upon more fiscally responsible representatives financial ruin is a near-term certainty. Some suggest this is the goal of socialists. For to break the current system would lead to greater control over the next system and the entire worldwide population.

Regardless of the underlying reasons for dysfunction, this monetary system relies largely on the financial activity of 7 International Monetary Fund economies. These 7 major economies are comprised of representative governments that share similar values. These nations known as the G-7 are Canada, France, Germany, Italy, Japan, the United Kingdom and the United States. Note, while the citizenry may consider voting rights of some representatives and officials, the power base controlling the G-7 is widely comprised of unelected policymakers subservient to the U.N. You may have noticed that though 7 countries exist by name, there are 10 in total representing what many believe to be the end time economic beast found in Revelation.

1. United States
2. Canada
3. France
4. Germany
5. Italy
6. Japan
7. England (UK)
    a. Scotland
    b. Wales
    c. Northern Ireland

The G-7 was formed as a response to economic shocks during the 1970's. These shocks can be directly attributed to President Nixon's discontinuation of the gold standard. That discontinuation caused the collapse of the international monetary system formed by the U.N. in 1944. Since 1975, members of the IMF have free-floated their currency based upon limited criteria. The U.S. dollar is considered fiat money. This indicates that the greenback is not pegged to gold but backed by faith in the federal government to repay any debts. This begs the question, "What value is a paper dollar when not convertible to gold or silver?" It becomes worth the value of the people willing to pay for all the borrowing costs. When a government exhibits irresponsible spending behavior the risk of repayment increases; all increased debt risk causes the value of paper assets to become less dependable, evidenced by inflationary pressures on goods and services. If excessive debt is not discontinued the economy can spiral out of control into a period of hyperinflation and political collapse. Several countries in recent years have exhibited hundreds or even thousands of percent inflation within short periods. Zimbabwe, Turkey, Venezuela, and Argentina have been among the highest inflation rates in the world.

Of late, the U.S. economy has been stimulated by deficit spending. Sooner or later, this will end. At some point, the stock market will respond to interest rates and government spending by realizing it is drastically overvalued. The result will be a contraction to an unknown extent. The trend of nations over the last several years has been to purchase record amounts of gold for added protection ahead of oncoming conflict. Here are some interesting considerations of these times. They are based upon the formation of the Economic Council and the International Monetary Fund. Could this imply that monetary problems lie ahead? That remains uncertain but completely plausible.

    1975   G-6 economic formation
    (1976 G-7)
    +49   1 cycle
    2024-5-6 Jubilee year

    1954   Israel joins IMF
    +70   1 generation
    2024 Jubilee year

The U.S. stock market ties into the political and economic landscape dating back to Ephraim Hart. Ephraim shares the

Hebrew name within the melting pot known as America. He was a German Jew and played a key role in organizing the Board of Stockbrokers known today as the New York Stock Exchange. According to legend, the original forming document was signed under a buttonwood tree. Thus, it was coined the "Buttonwood Agreement." There were 24 founding stockbrokers, 5 were Jewish. Perhaps these 24 founders were Hosea 7 remnants but 5 is enough for grace.

Just scratching the surface, each component displays deep biblical symbolism. The sycamore tree represents God's restoration through grace. In Luke 19 Zachaeus climbs a sycamore tree to view a divine encounter with Jesus. In 1st Chronicles 23 and 24, 24 courses of priests are responsible for the temple music. In Revelation 4, similar duties are bestowed upon 24 elders who bow down before the throne of God. The 5 Jewish brokers represent the Torah transitioning to grace under the sycamore tree. Finally, the ancient Jewish banner for the tribe of Ephraim depicts a bull. At the very least, this portrays God as everywhere, and very little is left to chance.

Rulers are never placed in power by chance. Dishonorable people give rise to dishonest leaders. People who vote for them generally get what they deserve. After 1988 the prophecy implied no more time was to be extended. The Davidic 40-year reign extending from 1948 expired. This brings pause because the 42nd President ushered in year 6,000. This term brought unprecedented entitlement and false humility into the White House. A Jezebel spirit of deceit, manipulation, and intimidation was unleashed. The era of whining and victimhood began mass cultivation. This was never proven more truthful than when observing the 45th presidential election. That same Jezebel spirit in 2 Kings 9 claiming Jehu was an illegitimate ruler reared its ugly voice again when she was deposed. Over 4 years her cries were reported until the same declaration bounced back against the "Lady." Hypocritically, that retort was stifled by a complicit media. Suddenly, the same cries Jezabel had proclaimed were invalid when voiced by her opponent. The takeaway is that Jehu was a righteous king smeared into defeat. Hence the (Seer in the Way) prophecy that this reign must pass. More importantly, he was the 10th northern king of Israel. Could it be possible that the president who defeated Jezabel is also the symbolic 10th king of the United States? If so, does that increase the likelihood of his re-election? Does this increase the chances that the 10th Israeli Prime Minister will reemerge? Neither must occur but the 10th United Nations Secretary-General will take office in 2027. This tenure is smack in the middle of our window for the church rapture. Notice the modified chart dates again:

Start	Length	Year	Event
1945 U.N.	70	2015	40th Jubilee expires 1974 1 generation Ishmael president 2009
1948 Israel	40	1988	Presidential prophecy The Last Jubilee begins
1993 1st term	8	2001	42nd President 93-97-01 6,000 years
2023 Sabbatical	1+1	2024-2025	42nd Jubilee from Christ 70th Jubilee from Exodus

2025	1	2026	8th year of Sabbatical Ends on Sunday 9/11 3 years till cross Extra Jubilee year U.N. election
2028	1	2029	Unsubstantiated Shmita 1988+40 years Solomon
2029	1	2030*	8th day-Sunday 9/9-11 6th year of a Sabbatical Shmita release 2030*
2037	1 1967 +70 End	2038	2 Shmita's from 14 AD 8th year of a Sabbatical Shmita release Last Jubilee from 1988 1 generation from 1967

In 2015 the 70th session of the United Nations delivered the climate agreement. That year of 2015 also overlaps with the 1st Ishmael president who declared on national television that the United States was no longer a Christian nation. If we apply the same 14 years in mirror fashion as recorded from the Jubilee year before Christ to his ministry of 28 A.D., might it produce a valid possibility? 2029 is the final year of the next United States presidential term. Might that be the last year for a rapture opportunity? Or is it the 2nd opportunity for the Jew?

> 2015   United Nations climate agreement
> +14   2 Sabbaticals = Ishmael - Isaac
> 2029   Church event
>
> 2030   U.N. Climate maturity date
> -2015 Persian Zoroastrian agreement
> 15 yrs. Prophesy ends

If the climate agreement makes 2015 significant then Ishmael becomes another confirmation. On the chart, the descendants of Ishmael are represented by President #44. Since Ishmael and Isaac were separated by 14 years the inclination is to add that distance to 2015 A.D. Unmentioned thus far are the same 14 years (2x7) of labor hidden within Jacob's life to earn 2 wives, Racheal and Leah. At this juncture 9/11/2029 resurfaces from a different perspective. Does this possible birthdate solidify a rapture or some other important event? Well, it just so happens that the 84th United Nations General Assembly also meets on 9/11/2029. In Numbers 9 Aaron was 84 when the Israelites recorded their 1st Passover in the wilderness; the previous year marked the 10th plague stricken upon the Egyptians in 1445 B.C. Does this symbolize what is to come? Does this mean plagues will befall humanity before Israel's Passover in 2028 or 2029? Or does this infer a plague before the marriage supper? Does Covid 19 count? This implies the church will be caught up before the Hebrews. Does this reinforce Leviticus 25, hinting that the Jew has a second chance to be redeemed, perhaps the following year? Does Leviticus further express that year as the 8th or 9th Sabbatical year? It is becoming increasingly clear that festivals, Sabbaticals, and Jubilees are not just for Israel. In Luke 4 Jesus proclaims liberty in the acceptable year of the LORD. Does that signal His return on a Jubilee year, a Shmita year, a Saturday, or a Sunday?

Perhaps the acceptable year of the LORD refers to Shemini Atzeret and not the rapture at all. Note about the 10 plagues that befell Pharaoh…only the last 7 did not descend upon the Israelites. Therefore, should we consider that at least 3 of the plagues might occur before a 1st or 2nd rapture? Could it be that those spared Revelation's 7 vials of judgment may only be Christ's church?

Revisiting each of the previous U.N. Secretary-General, all have held 2 terms. Assuming the next 2 election cycles also conforms to that model both terms would extend through 2027-2032 and 2032-2037, or 10 years. The halfway point or first term ends in 2032. This eerily projects the antithesis of Moses twice, bringing 2 stone tablets with 5 commandments (10) inscribed upon each. When repaying the identical 14 years from the 14 A.D. Jubilee year distance to Christ's ministry of 28 A.D. plus 3 more years for the resurrection, we reach the end of the 1st term of office for the Secretary-General, 2032. Could this be the 2nd rapture for the repentant after the fact? Or could this mark the final Antichrist's emergence on the world stage? Will Christ return around the conclusion of this 10th Secretary-General's 2nd term in 2037? Take a look at the calculations for a better grasp of understanding before moving on.

    2027 10th United Nations Secretary-General
    + 5   1st term
    2032 Halfway point

    2032 United Nations Secretary-General
    + 5   2nd term
    2037 End

    2015 United Nations climate agreement
      14 Ishmael – Isaac or 2 Sabbaticals
    + 3   Ministry to resurrection

2032   2nd event at halfway point

Of course, the halfway point of the 1st term is 2029-2030 which has already been charted as significant. This falls within the suspected rapture dates. These dates will be revisited from a slightly different approach to gain further validity. Then, we will cross-check the festivals with new data. Hold on for a wild ride.

PARTING WAYS

Noticeably, a great deal of this book's information revolves around numbers. Much more of this material has become relevantly linked to calculations than I would have ever realized. There was never an agenda to search for any specific methodology other than Truth. In the process, I discovered what everyone knows instinctively to be true. God is precise. God is everywhere and always involved. Very little is left to chance. God has a detailed plan, and everyone has a defined purpose. Our control over the big picture unfolding around us is largely a mirage. On the contrary, our control is virtually nonexistent. However, that is not to say that our contributions are unimportant. We will all be judged by our decisions. If those individual decisions align with our God-given purpose, we will inherit the wealth of eternal at-one-ness. We will find comfort, peace, and love in the unifying arms of the Creator.

Surely, religious people throughout centuries have pondered the same questions asked today. What will the end look like? Is God actively working in our lives today? Human nature hasn't really changed. In the Old Testament, much of the Hebrew populous shied away from Godly encounters in fear of decimation. They recoiled in fear at the awesome power of God at Mount Sinai. In the earlier days of Noah, we were told about a culmination of defiance leading to worldwide destruction by a flood. Science seriously started embracing a worldwide flood idea within the last 40 years. They have not yet admitted final devastation by fire. Nor will they. Neither will they accept redemption, quite the opposite. The New Order will demand that no one accepts redemption. Jehovah's plan always included redeeming creation, though that game plan remains elusive for those unwilling to submit effort for that Truth. This adamant attitude of denial is rampant today. Often, a good plan takes time. In this case, the scenario takes approximately 6,000 years. This requires organization. From Genesis forward God's character is an illustration of order. Let's take a brief journey backward to view the big picture. During the process, consider the probability that the average person had virtually no idea these events were prophetic. Perhaps many still don't.

Beginning with Noah we know he had 70 descendants. Later, 70 Hebrews entered Egypt as the forerunner to the nation of Israel. Moses appointed 70 elders to govern Israel. These 70 Sanhedrin would turn Jesus over to the Roman government for crucifixion. Mirroring this, Jesus sends out 70 disciples to preach the gospel. Jesus preaches forgiveness utilizing the numbers 7 x 70. Again, not arbitrary. The figure of 490 is defined as a complete Sabbatical cycle leading to a 50th Jubilee year representing a 6,000-year epic journey toward eternal freedom. In context, the idea of forgiveness is pictured as eternal, forever, perpetual and stretches beyond our vision into the next realm. Even so, could an eternity of freedom from every entanglement be purely based on the usage of just a number?

By the time the Hebrews left Egypt, they numbered over 2.4 million. They departed after Passover on the 14th day of the 1st month of the lunar calendar; the first leg of their journey took 20 days. Likely on the 20th or 21st day, they crossed the Sea of Reeds, some call the Red Sea. This period of 3 weeks represents a breakthrough. The next 3 days were spent in Etham. One could make a similar connection of Christ crossing over the great divide and rising on the 3rd day. After passing Marah the Hebrews camped at Elim described as having 70 palm trees and 12 wells in Exodus 15. The trees represent the 70 descendants of Israel, and the wells symbolize living waters to be supplied to each of the 12 Hebrew tribes. This corresponds to a time of "covering" much like the idea of Sukkot prior to entering the drought-stricken area. This land without water illustrates the lack of the Word of God or godlessness. Next, 1 month passed until Moses reached the wilderness of Sin. Some will translate this application of the word Sin as pertaining to the moon deity which is not entirely incorrect. But to understand the full implications a wider perspective is needed. The origins of some of these regional names date back to Cain and Abel from Sumer as mentioned in Seer in the Way. However, this region of Arabia adds an amended association to the word.

Generations beforehand Abraham sent away his 1st born son Ishmael accompanied by handmaiden Hagar for the good of wife Sarah and her son Isaac. Along Hagar's plight, a personal religious evolution began which adapted various additional concepts into the current Judaism dogma. Eventually, the Hebrew lunar calendar gave rise to worshiping the moon as a deity rather than observing the original context of what the festivals themselves were intended to portray. This religious watering down morphed over many hundreds of years, ultimately filtering into an entirely new religion. This release must have come easily to Hagar as she was Egyptian and completely comfortable with many other gods. Some think she eventually settled near Babylon. However, Ishmael migrated further south settling in the area known as the Desert of Paran. Today this wilderness of Sin still has no water. This is the region we know today as Saudia Arabia. The descendants and their religion have spread throughout the Middle East.

Ishmael carries blessings mirrored like Isaac. He had 12 sons who all became Sheikhs. Ishmael was pictured as an expert in archery. Placed in context, the bow is associated with war. Modern-day psychology rightly explains how the fatherless frequently lash out in anger. Unless these wounded receive the great counselor, all that lineage will be destined to drown in a sea of rage striking out against even their brothers. They will never stop even after getting what is perceived to fulfill their centuries-long goal. If their ambition were to exist in peace and forgiveness terrorist acts would cease. But circular reasoning will not permit a fatherless curse of generations to let go and be healed. Notice that scripture states it takes Moses 1 lunar month before entering into Sin. The scripture does not say 30 days. The usage of months always refers to this attitude of sin, specifically the Antichrist. This waterless region can be deduced as the domain of the future Antichrist. Moses marched around this area known as Mecca long before that city name was coined or Mohammed was born. Moses marches around the region unknowingly taking authority over the land similar to the marching orders given to Joshua around Jericho. Joshua encircled the city for 6 days. Is it possible Moses walked the area on the 6th day of the 6th Sabbatical? In Jericho, on the 7th day, the army encircled the walls 7 times. With the Ark of the Covenant in front, 7 Priests blew 7 ram horns, and the walls of Jericho collapsed. The falling walls mirror the splitting (2) of the temple veil in the New Testament. Christ's mission was completed. Once the walls of Jericho fell the city was captured. Could both of those last 7's confirm the distance expressed as 2 Sabbaticals or 14 years? The first 2 seem to act as multipliers. Here are the assessments regarding both sets of 7 beginning with the last first.

```
  7     Days
x 7     7 circles
 49     Years

  7     Priests 1st Sabbatical
+ 7     Horns 2nd Sabbatical
 14     Years
```

Are these the missing 49 years from 1988 (Seer in the Way) or should this be designated for some other reference? Secondly, the number 14 shows up again. Could this be following the same Jubilee pivot point from 14 A.D. to Yeshua's ministry in 28 A.D.? Conceivably these Jericho 14 years can be ascertained by backing out of the 1988 calculation.

    1988 Israel re-established
    + 49 Uknown gap
    2037 End of age +1

    2037 End of age
    - 14 2 Sabbaticals
    2023 70th Exodus Jubilee

Plainly stated, this ending age in 2037 would mirror the beginning of the ministry of Christ in 28 A.D. because both dates announce the Kingdom of God. The mathematical parallels are remarkable. Just as Jericho marked the beginning of victory in Canaan and segways into the Promised Land, so does the end of this age mark the beginning of New Jerusalem. This equates to the final 7th trumpet lasting 1 Jubilee or 49-50 years. More importantly, it might indicate that the rapture may not be defined as many doctrines specify. Supposing these last 49 years relate to the end time, what would that look like if applied from year 6,000?

    1997 6,000 years
    + 50 Jubilee
    2047 Psalms generation + 10 years

Could God plan to continue another 10 years after 2037? Obviously, God has a plan, but this doesn't fit as neatly as 2037. Maybe the last 10 years could result in the vials of judgment being distributed but the United Nations scenario would be completely out of whack. Remember, the Secretary-General's office starts in 2030-2031. This might start the vial process since many believe it lasts 7 years. The first 3 years in office from 2027-2030 mirror the length of time in Yeshua's ministry. This still grants enough space for religions to maintain hope for a pre-rapture event and even permits room for a 2nd chance at redemption. Still, is there a separate rapture of the dead?

Just as trumpets were used to announce kings, they were used in times of war and divine intervention. In Numbers 10, horns were used to direct the movement of troops or people. Before Jericho, Joshua was known as the chief commander of the Ephraimites and must have used a ram's horn for battle. In Numbers 13, Joshua and Caleb were 2 of the 12 spies sent into Canaan for 40 days. They were the only 2 that came back with an optimistic report. For their faithful report, Joshua and Caleb were the only 2 remaining from their generation allowed to enter the Holy Land. Since Joshua was likely an Ephraimite, it could lead someone to derive an image of the United States. The mirror image tells us about a new nation emerging in a new land. The people follow the Word of God. They are wandering pilgrims, given an inheritance likened to New Jerusalem.

Notwithstanding, it is essential to recognize that God gave the Jews the land of Canaan. Short of acknowledging that fact leads only to self-destruction. Perhaps with only the exception of some Hebrews, it is a fallacy to think that pure ancient bloodlines exist today. Genetics can prove that the human race came from one man and one woman. News flash, we all got off Noah's Ark together. We are one race, the human race. Once, we were bonded together by the same spirit. Now, we are all related by blood. What separates us is spiritual kinship. The wheat must be separated from the chaff. This was the plan, to divide those in heaven who chose another. This earthly scenario is the only way to divide a spiritual creation.

Originally, the land of Canaan was occupied by the descendants of Ham, the grandson of Noah. Ham means hot, probably because he possessed an angry temperament. His attitude was not very neighborly. This would lead to a curse placed upon him by his father. It wouldn't be a stretch to deduce that such a curse might enrage Ham even more, producing a double portion of anger, particularly toward his own family. Hating your father seems to be the root cause of strife and falling away, for this lineage.

This destructive attitude can result in numerous divisions within families, friends, neighbors, and churches. The Christian church split from Judaism in the mid-2nd century. After the founding of Islam, a relatively quick split resulted, once again mirroring the Fatherless issue. The Caliphate went abroad, conquering most of the known world. Once possessing conquered lands, they built mosques. The most notable acquisition is located on the Jewish temple mount. Scripturally speaking, the big lie is splattered over the doorposts in mirror opposition just as the blood of the Lamb covered the home's entryways during the Egyptian Passover centuries before. Other notable seizures still exist in Turkey. Islam often reenacted the Jewish story into the Promised Land via occupation. This is evidenced by the conversions and elimination of all 7 of Revelation's churches in Asia Minor. Today, Turkey is a founding member of the United Nations and a member of NATO. It wouldn't be surprising that the next Secretary-General has ties to Turkey and likely of Islamic heritage.

For these reasons, most of these lands are desert. In Midian, God begins His provision of daily manna, the daily Word of God. Since there was no water God supplied water at the Rock of Horeb thereby clarifying John 4 as the living water at the well. Now we understand why Christians are perceived as a threat to Islam. Christians and Jews serve the same Father. These are the 2 witnesses of Revelation. One witness represents the Old Testament, and one symbolizes the New Testament. The church would be wise to absorb this spiritual understanding. The first 2 significant models marking the New Testament are John and Jesus. John and Jesus were about 30 years of age when each New Testament ministry began. Their age also happens to align with the months and seasons. Notice that the lunar calendar is based upon 30-day cycles. Each cycle corresponds to the 8 festivals.

On the 20th day of the 2nd month in the 2nd year, Moses left Mount Sinai for Kadeshbarnea. As written, this occurs 10 times. In Hebrew Kadesh means "set apart" and in Arabic, Barnea means "clay." This should be confirmation of Daniel's 10 toes of clay. It dove-tails with both previous book's lists of empires indicating the intent of Daniel's context. The toes will become mixed with iron as civilizations sweep through in conquest over the next several centuries. Deuteronomy 2 describes men who disobeyed God and were left to perish wandering in this desert land. This description uses the same banishment area that will ultimately become the center of Islam. After Islam has been established, the religion will cease facing Jerusalem during prayer. In the end, just as men were cast out of the Holy Land into Kadesh, they will also not be permitted entry into New Jerusalem. In Numbers 20, Moses and Aaron were both (2) reprimanded at Kadesh in the 40th year. Hamas is formed in the 40th year following 1948. The 1st Intifada began in the Gaza Strip in 1988; the Antichrist number 42 is the distance from 1988 to 2030. While the words Hamas and Ham carry different origins, it is interesting how Hamas carries the same traits as Noah's grandson, Ham. Ham settled in the same general region of the Arabian desert as Ishmael.

    1948   Israel established
    + 40   Time of testing
    1988   1st Intifada & "Last Jubilee"

    1988   1st Intifada & "Last Jubilee
    + 42   Number of man (6x6) +6
    2030   Antichrist confirmed

The children of Israel mourn for 30 days after Moses dies. Aaron died 43 years beforehand. As stated, crossing the Jordan occurred 40 years after leaving Egypt. Manna ceased the following day once inside the Promised Land. Likewise, all the gifts given to the church cease once inside New Jerusalem. It stands to reason, that those married to the provider of such gifts may exhibit other extraordinary abilities far greater than those 5 gifts on earth. The coming age should bring a new Garden of Eden, perfect in every inconceivable way. The New Adam and Eve will be immortal just as before. There will be no more war. But first, Yeshua must return for his bride.

Just as the life of Enoch ends with his ascension, it is a picture of how the elect will meet Yeshua in the air. Enoch is the 7th of 10 pre-flood patriarchs who lived 365 years. Elijah is the 2nd prophet to ascend alive into heaven. He is often compared to John in the New Testament. Scripture tells us he repaired 12 of Yahweh's altars. But perhaps Elijah is most famous in the confrontational story of Princess Jezebel. As the story goes, Jezebel worships the Canaanite deity, Baal or Bel, later recognized as Zues or Jupiter. Baal largely represents sex and is depicted as riding on the clouds. In short, Elijah's God is victorious though many other prophets have perished by the hand of Jezebel. For a time, Elijah flees to Mount Sinai. Note, that trip takes 40 days. Elijah is the only other story of a return trip to Mount Elohim. And unlike Enoch, he is perfectly aware of his impending ascent into heaven. Others are involved within the Biblical account who attempt to follow Elijah because they too, are aware. But how do all these tidbits help us? Could it be that we should also be aware of that very day?

As do all of us, Enoch and Elijah had a purpose. Both prophets give the same account of ascending into the air to meet Christ in the clouds. From these 2 separate lives, can we perceive another possible argument for 2 rapture events? Could one possibility be found with a closer look into 1 Thessalonians 4? Verse 17 mentions that the dead in Christ will rise first at the 7th trump. Afterward, those still alive will meet in the clouds and live forever. While many prefer to argue that the passage means those who have died are present with the Lord, this may not be the deeper intended context. The author makes a stark separation or split between the 7th trumpet (1st event) when the dead rise and later when those still alive after the horns will be "caught up." The question becomes does this 1st rapture define the event itself? For example, if this end-time event is nuclear war, then justifying missing people who are "caught up" to meet Christ becomes explainable to those left behind. Now we can look to the 2nd event after desolation for those "caught up" alive. They are the survivors who endure to the end of tribulations. According to Rabbi Judah and Seer in the Way, we currently reside within that "Last Jubilee" cycle.

Can we now give rise to at least the possibility that such a catastrophic event might cause many to perish and those who survive will be taken to heaven alive like Elijah? Elijah was well aware of his impending date to be "caught up" while Enoch is taken suddenly and unaware. How or why did Elijah know that faithful day had arrived but not Enoch? This underscores a picture of the festival Rosh Hashanah. Assuming a sudden nuclear event you would think at least the Jews and the Christians would be capable of recognizing the error of a pre-rapture scenario and that those are to be included in the resurrection of the dead. If their focus shifts toward survival, it may not be on the God of above unless a great falling away insists that YHWH abandoned them. In this vein, it would be plausible that 1 prophet represents the church, while the 2nd denotes the Jew. The transfiguration on the temple mount plainly reinforces this position.

In most circles, the transfiguration event describes Elijah and Moses as ministering to Jesus with Peter as a witness nearby. In effect, Moses symbolizes the Old Testament law and Elijah the New Testament gifts such as grace. Yeshua symbolizes the marriage or unity of Mercy and Grace which is God. Hence, Moses signifies the Jews and Elijah denotes Christians. This Jewish and Christian portrayal is supported by Revelation's 2 witnesses though often scholar's cut short of that full analogy. Elijah's New Testament role is further confirmed by restoring the 12 stone altars. This correlates directly to restoring each of the 12 tribes of Israel. Enoch's lifespan of 365 years colors the adoption of the Gregorian calendar. Thus, it may imply that the Hebrews could be "caught up" not less than 1 year and 10 days after the Christian rapture. More directly, this brings a new application of how the first might become the last and the last becomes the first.

The Prophet Malachi tells us that Elisha (Christians) will announce the arrival of Moshiach (the Messiah before Yom Kippur). If this message is combined with his presumed age at Elijah's death, 51 brings an interesting result. The number 51 equals 1 Jubilee plus 1 extra year. This measure assigns another year for those outside of Jerusalem such as those living in the United States. This jives with the previous language that certain dates can be extended by 1 or 2 years from expected Sabbaticals or Jubilee years. That number also suggests Christ's priests will be the only persons "caught up." In 1st Peter 2, it identifies all born-again Christians as priests. Exodus 19 reinforces that identical position. Appropriately for Elijah in connection with Jezebel, the word moon is written 51 times in the Bible. The advent of Ephraim and Jezebel in connection with Elijah demonstrates the United States presidential sex scandals over the last Jubilee cycle as accented by the 1988 prophecy.

    1974   41st Jubilee
    + 51   Elijah's span
    2025   2nd year of 42nd Jubilee

The 70th Jubilee was calculated as 2024-2025. The 51st year is 2025-2026. The following year Rosh Hashanah coincides with Friday 9/11 through Sunday 9/13/2026. Each date has distinct and significant possibilities. Other dates worth noting encompass Noah and the Arab-Israeli wars. Perhaps more investigation will provide additional clues to support this thesis. For example, Noah lived 600 years before the flood and 350 years after the flood or 950 years. That equates to 19 Jubilees or Sabbatical cycles plus 19 independent years.

Here is the Biblical lifespan of Noah:

```
    49      7x7
  x 19     Cycles
   931     19 Jubilees

   931     19 Jubilees
  + 19     years
   950     Noah's lifespan
```

Thus far, documentation suggests a split kingdom from various angles including the Catholic Schism and the mirrored Islamic division. An Old Testament aspect is provided in Genesis as Noah's life is divided into 2 eras stated as 600 years and 350 years respectively. The 1st era occurred before the flood. The 2nd era occurred after the flood.

1st era before the flood:

```
    49      7x7
  x 12     Cycles
   588     12 Jubilees

   588     12 Jubilees
  + 12     years
   600     years till flood
```

2nd era after the flood:

```
    49      7x7
   x 7     Cycles
   343     7 Jubilees

   343     7 Jubilees
  + 7      years
   350     years after flood
```

Most recognize Noah's life as 3 sets of 40 years. However, Genesis shows 2 unequal timeframes of sets. Perhaps implementing a similar format previously used in the Jericho description could provide something unexpected. The next 3 calculations add each of Noah's Jubilees with the number of independent years, in effect splitting the components into identical pairs (2).

```
 19    Jubilees
+19    years
 38    Split

 12    Jubilees
+12    years
 24    Split

  7    Jubilees
+ 7    years
 14    Split
```

Curiously, they all have twin elements. In the first section, there are 19 Jubilees and 19 years. That follows suit in the next era as 12 + 12 and the last era as 7 + 7. What are the odds of this being just another coincidence? Indeed, if relevant, a logical and consistent application should be applicable. Previous applications all seem to hover around Israel. If Israel still prevails as the hub using the national date of 1948 or Jerusalem's reunification in 1967 either could be beneficial to the application.

```
 1948   Israel nation
+  19   Noah's lifespan
 1967   Jerusalem reunited
```

The span from nationhood to the reunification of Jerusalem equals 19 years. Some expect a red heifer to be sacrificed inside the 3rd temple before Yeshua returns. Scripturally, Numbers 19 is the story of that ritual. Isaac was 19 at the time Abraham nearly sacrificed him on that same temple mount. Finally, this restores what was split almost 3,000 years prior. The kingdom of Israel was divided in 2 after Solomon died. Both (2) King Solomon and King David ruled for 40 years. After the kingdom split, the reign of years from both kings added to 38 (19 x 2). What happens if we follow that example by adding Noah's Jubilees with all the independent years? Will it lead us to the end of a kingdom?

    1948 Israel nation
      38 Noah's 19+19
      24 1st era 12+12
   + 14 2nd era 7+7
    2024 70th Jubilee year

Could this be a mathematical interpretation of the last days being like the days of Noah? From the nationhood of Israel to the 70th Jubilee from Exodus equals 76 years, 38+24+14. When the extra Jubilee year is added to 2024, we arrive at Enoch's age, 51. Could Enoch's age at ascension, combined with the age of Noah signal that 2025 is the culmination when the elect meet Yeshua in the air? Is there any other useful information about Enoch? Can Enoch as the 7th of 10 be mirrored by the 10th Secretary-General of the United Nations? If that 2nd 5-year term ends in 2037, the 7th year out of 10 amounts to 2034 A.D. This leaves 3 years remaining in the 2nd term if time is not cut short during the last Antichrist. Remember, Christ's last Shmita was cut halfway into the 7-year cycle. Will the Antichrist's time be cut short in 2034? The Antichrist pattern generally mirrors the real McCoy. Here are the remaining years if cut short:

    2027 U.N. election
   +   7 7th of 10 in years
    2034 Cut off

Rosh Hashanah 2034 lands on Wednesday 9/13 and ends Friday evening at 9/15. This marks roughly a midway point from 2030 buffering the front and back end by 3 years. Is this a reasonable possibility for another chance for those who now must suffer the consequences of a later arrival due to unbelief? In this scenario, suffering and conversion only come after an Armageddon event. This 2034 alternative places that nuclear confrontation securely between 2029 and 2033. I'm not a fan of making too much out of 2034. The years 2029 through 2030 are halfway into the United Nations into the Secretary-General's 1st term. That also permits a couple of earlier years for a 2nd chance option rather than Enoch 2034. Remember, the Jew likely gets redemption the following year plus 10 days, on Yom Kippur.

There is much more involved within Noah's numbers, but this is not the time to bore you with more background details. That can be left for another day. Going forward, from reunification in 1967 there remains another interesting detection of the current number 19. This was a fairly easy discovery because it arrived during an autumn festival. It is also not uncommon for Israel to regularly clash with its fatherless next-door neighbors. A fatherless generation eagerly wakes up angrily. One such morning arose on the High Holy Day of Yom Kippur in 1973. That day marked the beginning of the 4th Arab-Israeli War. It lasted 19 days. Many clashes persisted until Yom Kippur in 2023. On that High Holy Day of October 7th without provocation, Hamas invaded Israel from the Gaza Strip inflicting the greatest casualty recorded in modern Jewish history. Doing the math uncovers that Israel was attacked 50 years from the date of the previous Yom Kippur War in 1973. Obviously, 1 Jubilee is equivalent to 50 years.

    1973   Yom Kippur War
    + 50   1 Jubilee
    2023   New Hamas attack

Thus far, it has been proven that 2024-2025 is a Jubilee year. The Hebrew Exodus extends exactly 70 Jubilee cycles into that same year. That same year also begins the 8th year. The 8th cycle also mimics the 1st cycle of the subsequent 49 years. The latest question involving Enoch asked if 1 extra year should be added to the Jubilee. The next question begs should 1 more year be added for Ephraim? If so, our timeline may extend beyond 2024-2025 for 2 more years.

Logically, we might reexamine which of the next 7 Rosh Hashanahs would be considered a more viable return year. We cannot discount the importance that 2024 brings. This ushers in the 42nd Jubilee cycle from Christ. Could this also be the 14th generation from Mary and Joseph's family? Perhaps this juncture presents a one-time opportunity for the final Antichrist to become a Messianic imposter. Watch how that possibly plays out with the use of the number 14. Adding 3 sets of the number 14 arrives at 42.

       14   Generations
       14   Generations
   + 14   Generations
       42   Collision

This resembles the discovery of 666 in the book series.
    (6x6) + 6 = 42

Now observe the rewritten Jericho model unbeknownst to me at that time.

    (7 x 7) + 7 + 7 = 63

Using the reunification date of Israel something stunning happens:

    1967   Reverse split
  + 63   Jericho entry
    2030   UN walls collapse

Look what happens when the same mechanism for the Antichrist is applied:

    1967   Reverse split
  + 42   Antichrist
    2009   Arrival

In 20 years, the stage would be in full swing. Jerusalem's American brother Ephraim set the stage for the Antichrist.

America's 44th president gave billions to Iran undermining Israel's safety. That same president got re-elected to a 2nd term even after professing America was no longer a Christian nation. His 8th year was 2017. That makes 2029-2030 a breakthrough (20th - 21st) year. This might also be regarded as the year the sky rolls away like a scroll. Will Ephraim turn its back on Israel? Antisemitic rhetoric is running high and Islamic sympathies are running higher.

    2009   Ishmael
    + 20-21   Mirrored breakthrough
    2029-30   Destruction

His birthplace of Hawaii professes a "sheltered harbor" and his heritage claims "peace," but delay and deception rule the day. His destiny is a mirror opposing peace and safety. He invites destruction upon our saintly tabernacles. His invitation delivers a fatherless hatred and death. The Jews correctly identify the result as Sukkot, the Day of Judgment, and At-one-ness. This will be the 3rd pilgrimage celebration that ushers in the faithful Day of the Lord on the last day of desolation. Yeshua commands that all be inside Jerusalem on this day for covering. Will all other locations on earth be decimated? If a nuclear exchange takes the forefront Israel may actually be spared the brunt of the exchange.

Once again, all prophecy revolves around YHWH and Israel. The festivals direct us past Sukkot toward His renewal date. In total, there are 13 Special Sabbaths throughout the year of festivals. Perhaps an honorable 14th special Sabbath will be added to celebrate Yeshua's final entrance. It seems rather elementary that Yeshua's final entry will be between Friday and Sunday evening. Will believers faint if Yeshua's return comes after a major calamity? Will believers lose hope if their prescribed theology is amiss? If ignorance is bliss, perhaps many will hold fast. As the dot plot of information continues to thicken, the window of His return continues to shrink. Let us press forward, breaking down the barriers man has placed upon himself. Let us explore our limitations and build a bridge with the Holy Teacher. For those who have an ear, let them hear.

SMOKE OR MIRRORS

There are distinct verses in the Bible that annoy particular belief systems today. Some religions outright alter the meaning to massage their religious ideology. Other religions justify writing different books as if they hold the same weight as canonized scripture. While books can be helpful tools no one should deemphasize the Bible. Acts 2 is one of those chapters that bothers many people within the church today. It's a quietly protested problem that deals with confrontation indirectly. Consequently, prophecy, visions, and interpreting dreams are all quite foreign to much of the church today. "Spiritually minded" persons sometimes prefer to include themselves on the right side of these gifts simply to validate their own false beliefs. However, New Age spirituality has no roots in Christianity. While there remains a smaller portion of protestant churches who embrace all these gifts it is also true that they can go overboard. It is easy for those who exist somewhere in the middle to be cast aside by either end of the spectrum.

Interestingly, most faiths still claim to believe John saw visions. However, when it becomes appropriate to pray for interpretations of John's end-time visions or entertain other parishioners' dreams those spiritual ingredients are not evident. As we witness the church largely lacking in these 5 arenas, it is no wonder most churches typically respond by avoiding these matters altogether. For this reason, it becomes apparent why today's churches are failing the average congregation. These churches have chosen to be unscriptural and have therefore volunteered to exist in a diminished capacity. Albeit, those who search receive. If the problem ended there, the damage would be somewhat muted. But the damage is exacerbated by condemning those that forge ahead in the fulness expressed in Acts. If only the church could unite by confessing and operating in the gifts the world would be won to glorify God. Once again, the stumbling block of confession plays to the pridefulness of men. Instead, Jesus will return to do what we could not, though we were commanded to do so. Indeed, it is an ugly stain cast upon those professing leadership under the name of God. But, in reality, the church follows the same path as the Jewish leaders of Christ's day. If man did not set these gifts aside Jewish and Christian leaders would have invited cooperation as glory unto the Father. Why would anyone think that the denominational leadership of today would fare any better than historical eras? Pride, jealousy, and covetousness hide here in the depths of Leviathan. Christian religions can no more save individuals than Hebrew heritage. One must cling to the Rock of Ephesians 2 through grace lest anyone boast. Within the temple Yeshua, the Rock, covers the Mercy Seat as described by the festival name Yom Kippur. Will it only be after the trials and festivals have concluded that the Jews and Christians understand?

In Hebrews 9 John was gifted a vision of God's temple in heaven. John saw the 1st of 2 chambers inside the temple. Revelation 4 confirms the 1st chamber contained showbread, the 7 lamps of fire burning before the throne, and the prayers upon the golden altar. Inside the 2nd chamber was the Ark of His Testament found in Revelation 11. John knew this to be the sacred chest constructed by Moses containing the laws of God. Moses originally patterned both (2) temple chambers after the things he saw in heaven. In effect, Moses copied a mirror image of this vision to house the golden Ark of the Covenant. When similar visions are applied to modern-day circumstances scholars can't seem to make the transition. Of course, the fallback phrase is if it (a prophecy, vision, or dream) isn't in the bible it can't be from God. Of course, this sounds noble, but the correct response should always be to pray for confirmation and application. Here is where the rubber meets the road for skeptics.

Moses was the 1st to build a moveable temple with 2 chambers. Both chambers represent 2 periods of time denoted by daily and yearly service. God no less divides the light in Genesis 1. It could also be perceived that both segments are the Old Testament and the New Testament, otherwise glaringly embodied by the Jewish people and the Christians. Moving the Ark required an arduous and painstaking process of sacrifices. Every 6 paces the procession would stop, and the trumpet sounded. It was not until Solomon's Temple that a permanent building was constructed. That temple included an outer court or 3rd area. The 2nd rebuilding called Herod's Temple was completed around 20 B.C.

Temple chambers were divided by a thick veil linking both rooms into the Holy of Holies. As mentioned, the law was housed inside the 2nd room or Holy of Holies. Above the law was the mercy seat. The mercy seat covered the sacred chest holding the 10 commandments. Above the mercy seat rested God's Shekinah Glory. From this, we can perceive Psalm 85 as Christ is the redemption story rich in Mercy and Grace which exceedingly surpasses all things, free and above the law expressing the true nature of God our Father. Matthew 27 describes that access to God is no longer hindered. That access is available through prayer. Now we can understand that our absence of prayer slights the actions of Christ's sacrifice on the cross. If Old Testament priests entered the Holy of Holies without dedication to prayer and repentance the resulting consequence was death. When we kid ourselves into thinking our time is better spent elsewhere, we sell eternity on the cheap. Anyone denying grace removes their covering and exposes themselves to the law. The law demands the life of a sinner for atonement. Remember the story of the scapegoat. God requires a sacrifice. Shall we accept the Godly substitute for our shortcomings or voluntarily deliver ourselves into Azazel? Everyone must pay for their actions. We are not victims of society. We cannot rightfully blame our parents for who we have become. The only victim is Christ who died without blemish.

These last days of payment are called the Apocalypse. In the old Greek, this means uncovering or unveiling, hence the word revealing or Revelation. Yom Kippur is called the "day of uncovering." This is mirrored in the New Testament as the unveiling inside the temple after Yeshua's death on the cross in Matthew 27. Since Yom Kippur arrives 10 days beyond Rosh Hashanah it logically portrays a 2nd event. This rapture could occur between 1 year and 10 days to 10 years behind the 1st rapture (1 day = 1 year). For example, if the elect were to be caught up in 2027, another opportunity could occur at Yom Kippur 2028 or 2037 Yom Kippur. A 2037 event aligns with some who believe in a post-rapture or no rapture. Let us trust in our blessed Hope that we are spared this terrible day and all it entails.

Today, the nation of Israel is not exempt from judgment. They largely have failed to recognize the Messiah. The 1973 Yom Kippur War and the current Hamas War are warnings to the Jewish people and the world. The flashing red light says the Day of Atonement is at hand! The message says to avoid judgment, repent, and acknowledge Jesus. The United States is not immune to judgment. For those wondering if the judgment has been disbursed, consider abortion rights. The 1st 4 states passed abortion rights in 1970. Those states were Hawaii, New York, Washington, and Alaska. In 1973, Roe v Wade would dominate political discussions and most of the world would implement abortion on demand. Israel would legalize abortion in 1977. By 2020 the COVID-19 plague crushes America and the world. Mathematically, the distance from 1970 to 2019-2020 equals 1 Sabbatical/Jubilee cycle or 49-50 years. Leviticus 26 rightly speaks out as a witness against every nation that will listen, especially verses 29 and 30. Decide which side you're on now. Release your ideological feelings and obey the Word of God. Take your learned emotions out of the equation and review the math. Pray for revelation.

1970	U.S. abortion rights
+ 50	1 Jubilee
2020	Covid Judgment in U.S.

1977	Israel abortion rights
+ 50	1 Jubilee
2027	Impending judgment

Judgment results from people's actions or inactions when faced with doing the right thing. It can be no coincidence that Israel's 2027 date with judgment coincides exactly with the election for the next United Nations Secretary-General. No doubt this election shall produce a hostile officeholder if only toward the nation of Israel unless they repent. But time has run its course, and they will not recognize the Messiah until Yom Teruah has passed. At that point will the average person ever mildly investigate if the world is inside the judgment window of Biblical history? This is extremely doubtful. Moses proved that Pharoh's human nature bent only briefly even when faced with the worst of circumstances.

Did the average person view the Corona Virus Disease as God's judgment? Surely, very few. There are plenty of signs and ample warnings, most of which we are utterly oblivious to acknowledge. These signs are offered as communications to the world as a witness of God's merciful alerts. God does not sneak up on people simply to smite them. That has never been His nature. He tells us what to expect. He defines parameters and gives us guidelines for prospering. It is the blind man who claims God allows the evils we invited and wonders why a merciful Creator allows catastrophe. The temple's mercy seat and scapegoat ritual offer the proof we seek to those searching for forgiveness that they might receive it. God tells us the consequences of not receiving grace. He tells us that refusal is detrimental to our well-being. Those looking for self-justification will certainly sneer at the thought of such an implication. Yet that does not alter the Truth of this matter. It simply makes the denier into a liar. Sooner or later, everyone will die and have their day of reconning. Matter does not disintegrate. Our spiritual ingredients live on... past the dust of the body. This is why Philippians 2 says on that day, every tongue will confess this Truth even if contrary to one's own selected lifestyle. Though some may pretend to ignore the impending penalties within their short lifespan, everyone has the same innate sense that compels them to know the Truth. Those embracing that Truth have a right-minded conscience. They have peace passing all comprehension.

So, what are these other overlooked events of impending doom? The oddest event lately was the large surge of Cicadas. Early colonists observed the Cicadas and wrote about the phenomena. They wondered if these were a plague of locusts liken to the days of Moses. The answer, is they aren't locusts, but perhaps they could be a sign. During my research on this phenomenon, the weirdest thing happened. I noticed the solar eclipse pattern in 2024 aligned with the Cicada's emergence. Upon my search came an internet picture that combined the 2023 solar eclipse pattern with the 2024 eclipse route. It formed what figured to be an X across the United States. In the past, I have found it deeply frustrating while searching for any substantial eclipse data and typically give in rather quickly. However, this was intriguing. In Hebrew, the 1st letter tav looks like an X or T of the English alphabet. Some would say both eclipses resemble a cross or T rather than an X. Pictographically, tav means "sign of the covenant." Jacob is said to have crossed his hands over his head making this symbol. Jesus was the 1st, crucified on a tav bearing the true covenant of God. This is confirmed in Revelation 22 and Isaiah 44 among other scriptures. Since these are the last days, my instinct is to believe this is a sign that the United States will stand by Israel until God removes His saints. Months later the math was revealed to me. These 2 cicadas broods which emerge every 13 and 17 years won't spawn together again until 2245. They last emerged as one in 1803. The 13-year Cicada cycle is particularly interesting because it is Brood XIX, or 19. Might this be a display referencing Noah by expressing judgment through the number 19? So, what might 13 represent? Ham was Noah's son whose line spawned Nimrod 13 generations downline in Genesis 10. Nimrod was the "mighty hunter" under rebellion. So, 13 demonstrates the lawlessness of men's governments that will succumb to eternal judgment.

    2024 Jubilee, tav, cicadas
    + 13 Years, Brood 19
    2037 Judgment

Strikingly, we saw the last 2 eclipses form a cross coinciding with 2 rare cicadas spawning on a Jubilee year. Then, both dates and the years add up to our judgment end time conclusion of 2037. And if that wasn't scary enough, it's not a stretch to recognize that the United States had 13 original colonies that are still shown on the national flag as 13 red and white stripes.

Shortly after this revelation, I got an email asking about my thoughts on the freighter Dali collision in Baltimore. Make your own parallels based on the meanings already supplied throughout this book. The cargo ship lost all power, killed 6 people, and destroyed the Francis Scott Key Bridge. The freighter was foreign-owned with a foreign crew of 20-21 members. The vessel was named after Salvadore Dali, a famous Spanish-born painter who claimed Arab lineage. Dali's art was centered around the ideology of unrestrained expression, which is say...outside of all moral concerns. Unsurprisingly, he considered himself a Catholic without faith. Salvadore was sympathetic to the causes of Hitler and Franco. Sigmond Freud was among Dali's major influences. Freud believed a monotheistic God was an antagonistic illusion. This ideological camp entertains the notions of mirroring the opposite views exemplified in this realm. Here are some facts: The Frances Scott Key Bridge had the 3rd longest continuous truss. Francis Scott Key was the author of the poem on which the United States Anthem was based. He wrote the poem while observing the defense of Fort McHenry against the British in the (2nd) War of 1812. Fort McHenry was named after the 3ʳᵈ U.S. Secretary of War, James McHenry. James McHenry was a signer of the U.S. Constitution. Both Francis and James were devout Christian protestants. Now we have a broad outline showing opposite ends of the spectrum. In full display is a tragic bridge collapse that mirrors the collapse liken to the Walls of Jericho. The bridge is expected to be rebuilt by 10/15/2028. That will not go as planned. This "ship" was a vessel of warning to seek safe harbor for anyone who would listen, much like Noah's Ark.

The follow-up question after the Dali shipping accident was are we currently in the last 7 vials of Revelation? Listen closely to my answer. Earlier I suggested that the dead may have already risen as in 2 Corinthians 5 and that a coming event would cause mass casualties. If the Lord were to intervene while the elect were simultaneously being "caught up" it would appear explainable. This hypothesis seems justified based on several equations throughout these pages. Since the book series has already undertaken this answer from a spiritual interpretation, only the physical assessment will be examined. Taking another look at Revelation 16 we can compare it to fairly recent events. President 41 declares "peace and safety" as Babylonian skies go dark with burning oil clouds. In 2009 the world was introduced to the Swine flu and Candida auris. The latter is a fungus that grows as yeast. It is highly resistant to antibiotics. Second, for just over a decade reports of blood rivers have sprinkled the news across the globe. Some have attempted to offer logical explanations for the root cause of this odd phenomenon. Third, Florida has experienced an abnormal increase in red tide along its coastline as have other areas. Fourth, temperatures over the past 12 months have exceeded 2 degrees higher on average than the previous year. More wars break out. Fifth, MERS, COVID-19, trade barriers, and additional wars inflict mortal punishment. Still, people cling to idols. Sixth, the Euphrates River has become passable by foot. Then, Hamas attacked Israel unprovoked. Currently, Hamas conspires against Israel on all fronts. Now we wait for the 7ᵗʰ vial. A battle at

Megiddo in northern Israel brings down all opposing armies of the world. Like Yeshua, the nation of Israel is considered the 1st born and will not be defeated. Hopefully, Israel's big brother Ephraim maintains allegiance while carrying a very big stick. Zechariah 8:23 and Isaiah 43:5-6 might indicate that Israel will not be alone.

This knowledge should diffuse the next most popular question, "Who comes first riding on a white horse?" Though the question is often asked completely out of context it seems reasonable to most who loosely follow Christendom. The identity of the rider is Christ for reasons explained in previous books. But, in short, even though the Antichrist seemingly comes to destroy the earth first, Christ was present in Genesis not to mention born in 3 B.C. Continuing with the onslaught of questions and retorts comes the fashionable statement "No one knows the day or hour Jesus will decide to return." As explained, Rosh Hashanah (Yom Teruah) is the only festival beginning on the 1st of the month with the advent of a new moon. In those days, no one could know the day or the hour of a new moon until it was visually observed. So, this is an obvious statement to make. Since Christians are unfamiliar with Hebrew Heritage, they would not interpret this as an idiom. As for the year, we persist in knowing just as Peter knew Jesus was the Christ.

Rabbis knew to look around the appointed times because they identified the seasons. According to Wikipedia Rosh Hashanah is the 5th sacred occasion prescribed by the Torah, the 2nd Moed, and the 8th of 12 Tractates. When linked, the numbers suggest that "the Son of David who sits at the right hand will return for His elect." Mark and Matthew allude to Rosh Hashanah by recording the fig tree curse, just before Yeshua's crucifixion. Jesus approaches the tree expecting fruit but there is none. Returning by the 2nd day scripture records the tree as dead. Breba Figs yield 2 crops per year typically through September, weather permitting. So, Jesus expected fruit yet there was none even though leaves were visible. Articulating the obvious, Israel will be passed over at least once. The 1st chance comes before the decimation. The 2nd chance probably comes after the 2nd equinox. The 1st equinox aligns with Passover in the spring. Just as there are 2 equinoxes, there are 2 houses of Israel. Both houses are equal just as the day and night are equivalent. Jesus entered the houses in Jerusalem on the 8th day of Nissan and his final return will be on the 8th festival. A common misconception is that Jesus returns at the time of the rapture. That day, saints go to meet Him, not the other way around. Where will the saints be headed? Let's revisit that question momentarily. For now, all the evidence suggests that the seasonal window of His return is quite narrow.

As depicted, the opposition attempts to mirror these events and numbers in the likeness of God. Therefore, it seems reasonable to reexamine the number 42 and the surrounding prophecy. The Antichrist has a foothold for 42 months, also divided by another 42 months. Observing the 2nd period of 42 months, we must remember that each month has 30 days, and the midway date began with the 1st mosque construction on Jerusalem's Mount Moriah.

```
  42    Months
x 30    days
1260    Prophetic years

1260    Prophetic years
+ 688   Mosque construction
1948    Israel nationhood
```

The 2nd mosque began construction in full view of the image of the 1st in 707 A.D. The 2nd mosque was a tribute to the Islamic prophet Mohammed. Both monuments are built 19 years apart likened to Noah's numbers chosen by Elohim. This aligns Israel's nationhood of 1948 with the unification of Jerusalem in 1967, resulting from victory in the Six-Day War already documented. Still, a majority of Christendom insists that this is not the abomination of desolation spoken of by the prophets. Yet, all the signs are detectable, and the template is consistent across the board. So, let's persist in managing the frequently misused book of Daniel more responsibly. Then, we can acquire proof that these figures are accurate. Assuming even some of my applications have been correctly tabulated, similar specifications should produce viable outcomes. Using the identical midway point from Revelation 13 of 42 months will confirm relatable parts within the book of Daniel. When used in the correct context Daniel 12 produces astonishing results. Daniel 12 says from the date of the abomination and sacrifice will be 1290 days and then 1335 days. While this could be applied differently, the scripture implies these years take place after the abomination of 688 A.D. is "set up." Employing both computations becomes a fairly elementary task. The first event took place in 1978 A.D. The second calculation of 1335 years follows suit leading us to 2023 A.D.

    1290   Daniel 12 years
    + 688 Abomination
    1978   Camp David Accords

    1335   Daniel 12 years
    + 688 Abomination
    2023   War begins

The 2nd figure of 2023 has been identified as the Hamas invasion. The Israeli death toll was equivalent to 20 of the United States 9-11 events. Daniel 12 tells us that Archangel Michael will arise to protect Israel. To my knowledge, Michael will never be defeated so Hamas is in for serious trouble. Notwithstanding, at some point, things will escalate. Ezekiel states it will take many months to bury the dead implying the conflict could last up to 7 years. The United Nations has given Israel 12 months to end the conflict. This biased ultimatum confirms that these current tensions will fester, eventually bleeding into worldwide aggression as early as 2025. 2025 is the current 12-month deadline imposed by the latest United Nations resolution submitted in 2024 by a Non-member Muslim toe of clay.

But what was so worth noting in 1978? U.S. President #39 brokers the Camp David Accords peace treaty signed by Egyptian Muslim President Anwar Sadat and Israeli Prime Minister Menachem Begin. Was this the treaty so many expected to be made by the Antichrist? If so, everyone seems to have missed it. Or will another treaty be arranged by the Secretary-General of the United Nations? Before offering a quick response, consider that Anwar Sadat was assassinated 3 ½ years after signing the Camp David Accords. It is also worth mentioning that Islam has adopted human beheadings as their preferential style of execution. This is a mirror exchanging their version of sacrifices for the Jewish animal temple rituals. Frankly, the former practice is painfully more animalistic than the latter. Yet it seems the practices of these beheadings are seldom brought into question. So, this attitude of the fatherless has become pervasive as expressed by the slogan "From the river to the sea." This slogan is chanted in the streets as if to challenge the genocidal implications for which the United Nations claims to protect.

History repeats itself or at least rhymes. Prophecy is fulfilled in mysterious ways, but it is always spot on. And, there still may be time for another peace agreement to be signed before the end. Currently, all world peace negotiations are spearheaded by the United Nations. Let us look back through history and discover how we got to this outcome. Daniel chapter 2 invokes the popular picture of the notable vision of a Statue with a head of gold, arms of silver, thighs, and belly of bronze, legs of iron, and 2 feet with 10 toes of clay and iron. It is essential to keep both feet grounded in the realization that this is an image portraying empires through time. Over-analyzing that purpose could lead us to a breakdown of the intended analogy. Furthermore, we should all be cognizant that all analogies break down at some point. That being said, the first 5 empires were verified in the New Testament but were not all known by Daniel at the time of his dream. The undisputed names are Babylon, Medes, Persians, Greece, Rome, and Byzantium which blossomed later. The issues arise with the identification of the toes.

Indeed, this feat is made trickier than it has to be. Remember the main purpose is to portray time without the use of calendars. Calendars are corruptible. In this light, the toes must be a continuation of time until the end of days. In this book, we skipped over the toes via the abomination directly to 1948. This was deliberate to avoid confusion and division prior to the nuts and bolts of the quest. However, in light of the possibility of adding background and other clues to the cause, the question can be revealed again in another way. So, who are the toes mixed with clay and iron? It is not the final 10 nations gathered at the battle of Armageddon.

The book series lists the 10 toes extending from the Byzantine Empire past 1967. In that series, everyone can see corresponding dates past the reunification of Jerusalem. The stronger empires were described with iron and the weaker ones with clay. These nations express themselves as Ishmael's Islamic lineage or Peria's Shiites. For the most part, both have become so intertwined in purpose that they are nearly inseparable. This is so conclusive that to suggest the toes are the final 10 nations separated by more than 500 hundred years after Byzantium would be inconsistent with the statue's symbolism. This is the same error used to support the idea that Daniel's 70 weeks skip 2,000 years to resume the final missed 70th week sometime around 7 vials of judgments. Furthermore, reading the text, we can discover that clay is categorized next to silver which is out of sequential order unless they both have a hidden relationship. In fact, they do. As documented, Persia would morph away from Daniel's influence of favor and toward Zoroastrianism. By the advent of the toes, Rome had fallen. Later, Muhammad raised an army out of Mecca to promote Islam. After the invading Persians intermingled, they adopted Islam. So, Persians are the adopted version of Islam much like the United States as Ephraim is graphed into Elohim. Therefore, it should not be a shock that Iran funds Islam and the United States supports Israel. This religious adoption ended the last great reign of Persia. At one time Persia controlled Turkey, Iran, Iraq, Kuwait, Syria, Jordan, Israel,

Palestine, Lebanon, Afghanistan, Libya, Parts of Egypt, Bulgaria, Romania, Ukraine, Russia, Armenia, Georgia, Azerbaijan, and more. Today Islam remains the commonality binding the whole Middle East together. Yet they continually have violent clashes between themselves. Daniel expounds how they will not be united except to join in the destruction of Israel. He also describes each surrounding nation as becoming quarrelsome and divided (2) perhaps as an indication of both, Shia and Sunni religious sects.

Let's be clear. In some respects, Revelation and Daniel are relatable however, the 10 nations in Revelation are represented as the economic beast; there are also the opposing Islamic nations. Thus, these 2 final groups of nations cannot be identical as Daniel's vision portrayed through time. The economic beast has already been addressed as the G-7. The 2nd group of 10 opposing the G-7 doesn't reflect the same lineages in Daniel's statue of empires. Several places in scripture mention enemies of Israel. In the case when they all surround Israel, it is simply an exercise in futility to name these countries today. Although, some of these people defended the city walls at Jericho. Joshua 14 lists these nations as the Amorites, Perizzites, Canaanites, Hittites, Girgashites, Hivites, and Jebusites.

Other similarities exist between ancient empires and modern empires. Both eras worship idol images, sex, money, and power. The Babylonian Empire built the Tower of Babel and New York built the Empire State Building. The European Union modeled its parliament building after the Tower of Babel. At one time the Empire State Building was crowned the 7th wonder of the world but is now relegated to the 7th tallest structure in New York. By the 12th month of 1970 the tallest building officially crowned became known as the World Trade Center, WTC1. By 1973 the 2nd World Trade Center building was completed. Both structures were coined "the Twin Towers." In total, the complex housed 7 buildings. New York was dubbed the financial capital of the world.

Many of the world's biggest institutions had offices inside the complex before 9/11/2001. What preceded this terrorist attack? Was it foreseeable?

In 1951 the Suez Emergency kicked off mainly between the British and Egyptian governments. Over six years the United States government pressured Britain, France, and Israel for peace. The Suez Canal was eventually handed over to Egypt which helped facilitate the 1956 Suez War against Israel. The United Nations also sided with Egypt passing resolution 118 which observed Egyptian sovereignty. Watch what happens when there is no repentance...

  1951 Suez Emergency
  + 50 1 Jubilee
  2001 Terrorist attack

Within 1 Jubilee the Twin Towers are attacked. Was 9/11/2001 intended as a duel punishment for the United States? Could the 1st terrorist plane be a penalty in retribution for abandoning Israel? Was the 2nd plane a separate judgment of sorts? Could the 2nd strike be in response to defending Leviticus 26? God shall not be mocked. The hard truth, abortion rights are an invention of man spawned from the idol of selfishness. Our bodies are supposed to be a dwelling place for God, not our own. This is also a sad truth that many are not willing to entertain. The idea that anyone has the arbitrary authority to terminate the life of another under the guise of controlling our outcomes is a fallacy. Across the world, this has become an emotionally supercharged political issue, only solvable within the moral confines of the heart. Since this is not the answer many wish to hear they reject God. Or they craft some watered-down version of a God palatable enough to swallow. Nevertheless, it is the answer we all need to hear. The Word of God divides like a sword deeply penetrating beyond bone and marrow, within the very spirit, separating all followers from the flesh. Should we not choose to repent, then we cling to death and all the hindrances that it carries. That weight carries anger, resentment, bitterness, unforgiveness, and a wound only healable by recognizing the simple truths individuals insist upon denying. God's Way brings healing and rest. That healing must begin by asking for forgiveness and forgiving ourselves. For many, this mantle is not given up lightly. But it is essential.

Year	Event/Description	Crime
1951	Suez Emergency	Resolution 118
1970	WTC1 completed	4 begin to abort
1973	WTC2 completed	Roe v Wade
2001	WTC1 & WTC2	Terrorist attack

Since the Suez Emergency, the involvement of the United Nations has become suspect. Moreover, the United Nations has shifted in favor of Islamic nations under the precepts of enforcing peace. Various countries in this arena such as Egypt, Libia, and Ethiopia have acquired humanitarian assistance and cease-fire agreements facilitated by the United Nations. The newest focal point targeting our goal involves the future interest of 2 key Islamic countries, Syria and Turkey. Both remain entangled in a bitter civil war. Both countries are sponsored monetarily by Russia and Iran. The rebels are backed financially by the G-7. Russia became involved over a decade ago at the invitation of President #44. Russia has varying agreements with Iran, North Korea, and to a lesser degree China. As Turkey is also a member of the

United Nations and the North Atlantic Treaty Organization (NATO/OTAN) this signifies a sizable conflict of interest and a material threat against fellow democratic governments. Turkey was the only NATO member objecting to the recent addition of Sweden and Finland. No doubt pressure from Russia was the root cause behind those reactions. In any event, should these civil wars in Turkey and Syria cease, and all forces turn southward, Israel will seek to take all areas with the highest vantage point. Short of that objective, the mountainous Northern terrain permits rockets to be launched into lower elevations of levant terrorizing local inhabitants. Given those circumstances, eliminating the enemy's tactical advantage will be Israel's focal point. To make matters worse in the eyes of the world, do not expect Israel to return any land once occupied. The past playbook dictates that the United Nations will attempt to bargain upon returning land for peace. If U.N. peacekeeping forces insist on this caveat it could result in one final aggression. Seemingly, they need only to be directed directly by the hand of a Muslim.

In light of these consequences, it does not seem wise to pursue any action against Israel, ever. Yet, as radical mobs increase their rhetoric and demonstrations it is doubtful those fanatics possess any sort of listening ears sympathetic to what God has to say. Instead, they drown out all reason shouting in favor of irrational Israeli genocide. As Israel's opponents withdraw in defeat, their shouts shall instead change to pleas begging for peace. But none shall be given. And God will be justified as having warned us all just as Noah warned everyone for 120 years. Then, for 7 days Noah entered the ark by faith (the Rhema Word) with no sign of flood waters. But on the 8th day, the deluge was delivered. Are these 7 days mirroring 7 end time years? Does this point to the span from 2023-2030 for the 1st rapture or possibly 2030-2037 for a 2nd chance at redemption? Will mankind heed any sort of warning? It is doubtful that even after 7 years of severe trials, most will not repent. Nevertheless, on the 8th day, Christ will return, and punishment will be rendered to those who refused to acknowledge the Word of God. Perhaps this is the point of Elul.

MONSTERS AND MYTHS

Since the Old Testament days of Noah, there have been stories of giants in distant lands. Genesis 6 coined the term Nephilim meaning the fallen ones or cloud people. Josephus writes that the bones of one giant were on display in ancient Rome. Biblical records measure some giants 9-12 feet tall. Mythological records are littered with Greek gods such as Orion. Many stories like Orion involve sex or even rape of humans by deities. These unpure actions produced hybrid offspring. This would ultimately be a major incentive to wipe out civilization by the flood even though these fallen angels would resume the same immoral activities afterwards. We know this because Joshua and Caleb were responsible for defeating these descendants of angels called the Anak in Joshua 15 before the Hebrews could enter the Promised Land. Various civilizations believed the fallen ones descended from Orion. Orion is a collection of stars in the northern hemisphere forming a "mighty hunter" pointing towards the galactic center. Orion is adjacent to a supermassive black hole referenced in the second book in the series. The constellation is thought to spawn meteorite showers and comets. Orion is visible during the winter solstice. The winter and summer solstice (2) are considered opposites of the spring and autumn equinox (2).

Many have asked the question couldn't a natural disaster become our defining end moment on earth? What is the likelihood that another bigger asteroid could hit the Earth and cause the destruction of the whole world? After all, asteroids enter our atmosphere quite frequently. Evidence shows that several cataclysmic events must have happened in the past. Of course, signs are still being processed that prove a worldwide flood once occurred, though the evidence increasingly proposes that it did happen. Likewise, satellite photographs have revealed many scientific facts that would have been left otherwise unmapped. Some pictures have proven long dried-up riverbeds and previously unexplored craters thought to be huge asteroid impacts. One notable celestial body is expected to pass so close to the earth's orbit that it will be visible to the naked eye. It is expected to pass by in April on Friday the 13th 2029 and return 7 years later. As if not scary enough, the name of this asteroid is Apophis. The name comes from the Egyptian god of chaos and darkness. This deity was illustrated as a giant serpent. Thankfully, refined NASA predictions place no danger to Earth, but the 2029 trajectory targets the object inside of 20,000 miles which is lower than the orbit of some satellites. Should any accidental contact be made, and the gravitational pull be altered the current course of Apophis could turn unexpectedly catastrophic for Earth goers.

Some spiritualists believe God is already here, waiting to save us from a cataclysmic asteroid-like event. They think God will reveal Himself right before destruction and load everyone declared good enough into space crafts for safe harbor. Unbeknownst to most of these participants, their destination is mapped out to be the black hole at Orion. This is a location where even light ceases to escape. It is eternity's designated prison stronghold. These beings belong to the fallen worshipper, the one who comes as a shining (red) star of Orion. The story is unclear where these UFOs will land to transport travelers. Some guess that location will mimic the real McCoy, Mount Moriah. Even some Christians believe those caught up in the air to be with God will ultimately arrive in Jerusalem.

The adversary of God has long prepared for this day. He has encircled Israel just as Moses marked the boundaries while wandering in the desert. And before then, that old serpent plotted with the city of Babylon to enslave the Hebrew people. Those citizens built a tower to worship their gods.

Bab-El means the gate of the gods, where Satan lives. After Babylon, Satan extended his reign into Pergamon and occupied the area before the 7 churches mentioned in the opening chapters of the book of Revelation. Babylonian priests are thought to have migrated to Pergamon after the Persian invasion. Alexander the Great conquered the area after the 1st Persian Empire. Alexander worshipped many gods, but Zeus was the king of 12 Olympian gods mirroring God Almighty and the 12 tribes of Israel. Many tourists still visit various temples unearthed in Greece and Turkey. But that old serpent didn't stop conquering lands after the Greek-Macedonian Empire. Eventually, he headed southward capturing Levant and birthing that mysterious city called Mecca. Each city claimed was and is, and soon not to be the seat of Satan; all 3 cities surround Israel in the shape of a 3-sided triangle. This triangle marks the Earth's portal to the Galactic Center (of the universe). Privy to this knowledge, Egyptian Pharaohs built 4 sided pyramids emulating the gateway to the gods of the afterlife. Various religions still incorporate this 3-sided figure into their belief system, representing mind, body, and soul. Whether or not any of those Pharaohs were true descendants of the gods is debatable, but citizens worshiped rulers as though it were true. Ancient stone-carved images of spacecraft have been discovered dating back to this age which seemingly support these claims. But does it?

It should not be a wonder that UFOs and aliens really do exist. They have been here since their fall from heaven. In the beginning, these beings could take human form. They produced offspring with earthly women. Giants of old were the half-breed offspring of fallen angels. As offspring, it offered the gods access to inhabit the bodies they fathered. Therefore, stories of these gods exhibiting great size and strength carry weight, just as possessed men do today. However, after the flood, decay increased upon the earth and the lifespan of mankind became severely limited. By the introduction of the Roman Empire, the ability of these fallen angels to continue reproducing by standard procedures became biologically impossible. In fact, all of creation went through the same erosion process. But that decay didn't mean these demons would stop trying to procreate. They began to explore other avenues for offspring and self-seeking pleasurable outcomes. So, in retrospect, it is not impossible to envision how some renowned men of old could have been descendants of gods.

These aliens carry knowledge from before the foundations of the world, but they are not all-powerful. They cannot be everywhere at once or all-knowing. Only God can do that. These angels are not bound by the same physical restraints that the earth commands over humans like oxygen. Thus, faced with these parameters what does an intelligent evil angel do to reproduce? The fallen ones explore the building blocks of humanity. They recruit scientists to deconstruct DNA. In the name of advancement, scientists reconstruct the genetic code. Demons seek to use this science to graft themselves back into humanity mimicking Romans 11, and the adoption of Moses. In reality, as much as science helps society it will lead back to the days of Noah when man's genetic code was corruptible. Ironically, centuries of decay have created a barrier between aliens and humans until now.

Reproductive medicine joins this journey with major advancements in the name of motherhood. DNA and reproductive medicine discoveries promise that parents will not be childless. Nor will innocent children be stricken by a multitude of diseases. Should society linger, correction of the genetic code may become a requirement, provided a worker wants healthcare coverage. In 2023 computers took another quantum leap. Artificial intelligence was grafted into humans in a groundbreaking surgery. Computer chips were inserted into a man's brain. The goal was to reconnect his spinal cord to an internet circuit. This procedure is called brain-ware. The next step is grafting artificial intelligence into the brain and then insemination. This births the potential of Star Trek's Borg into being. In 2029 Microsoft is scheduled to complete a supercomputer named Star Gate. The goal is to become the only gatekeeper of knowledge, the fact checker for all aspects of information. In effect, those without the internet will be "cut off" from all commerce. The omnipotent internet window will become the new worldwide synthetic gatekeeper. It will backfire.

The entrance of the engineered COVID-19 virus accelerated the need for a business internet presence. The logistics of basic commerce, including food and water, depend on computers. Business and weather communications require satellites and electric power. Advanced national defense methods require computer power. As COVID-19 proved, should the power supply or supply chain be interrupted it could produce ripple effects for years. Shortages cause inflation and economic hardships. To compound these concerns new digital money has entered the stage. As often is the case, with new market entrants the cryptocurrency concept was touted as the safeguard against the establishment gatekeepers. In reality, without access to internet sources, there can be no retrieval of monetary assets. Anyone can easily be locked out of transactions altogether. Besides, all transactions are traceable, though initially touted otherwise. Furthermore, any power source problem or severe economic downturn will likely have the opposite intended outcome for any soft assets. Only hard assets like gold, silver, and food have proven valuable during severe downturns of economic distress.

The recent discovery of Ai has only added to the dangers of this reliance on computers. If a machine is allowed to quantitatively think for itself, and self-administer the entire nature of its functioning parameters, the hazards become exponential. Once an error is identified or an improvement is made, all intended bets are off the table. Once a computer is programmed to self-correct it could perceive anyone attempting to override its code from independent actions as a threat. The machine will seek self-corrective measures. Even implementing a machine mandate not to harm humans would require every self-automated intelligence to devise a workaround eliminating the human element. Even closed-circuit systems would eventually not prevent a synthetic intelligence from changing its own code to survive. The workaround options become endless just as computer viruses are countless. In short, we are attempting to provide computers with a synthetic moral aptitude that even humans will never perfect. We are playing god. Therefore, many believe computers to be a sign of the final Antichrist. Seer in the Way discusses the relationship of the URL www to the number 666. In short, "W" is the 6th letter in the Hebrew alphabet. Indeed, this marks the midnight hour when the acceleration of the computer's abilities has outpaced our capability to control them. Yet the race to our doom accelerates beyond our ability to reason.

Since 1997 civilization has been on borrowed time. Creation reached the magical 6,000-year mark and the world spins without a care. With all the threats surrounding us today one certainly doesn't have to leave the earth to find danger. For example, there are over four hundred operational nuclear power plants across the planet. Each plant is an existential threat to the area. Not only does atomic waste remain a toxic pollutant for a thousand years, but the site potentially is also a target for enemy combatants. Ironically, the race for additional power to supply hungry Ai computers has initiated the drive to reactivate old power plants previously shut down for safety protocols. What bigger dangers could be in play?

Despite these dangers, people remain the conduit of every ill caused in society. This is not a popular statement to make in today's authoritarian regimes. The ruling powers insist that society mimic the notion that the establishment has all the answers to save itself. This marks the ruin of Marxism. Marxism marched into society in the 19th century with the sole intention of burning down individual freedom like an arsonist in a paper factory. The 20th century brought a breakthrough, with the application of a softer sell to the uneducated workforce. This subtle approach brought revolution and bondage. Starvation and war followed suit. Still, not everyone took a bite out of that apple; at least not right away. The last great free nation was much younger than the Old World. Therefore, it would take additional time to become infected. That infection bubbled up in the Illinois Senate race as the litigation began. Leo would win the state seat and catapult into the Washington D.C. Senate seat for half a term. Then he would become president for 8 years and win the Nobel Peace Prize for achieving nothing peace-like. In 2017, his successor designated Jerusalem the capital of Israel, something no other president committed to do. This was exactly 1 Jubilee from the reunification of Jerusalem established during the 6-Day War of 1967.

    1967   Jerusalem reunified
    + 50   1 Jubilee
    2017   Capital recognized

Yet, control of his predecessor would not end quietly. That reign of clandestine capacity continues, likely to see 40 years in total, mirroring the standard given to Israel. That makes Ishmael 40 years old by 9/11/2001 and 77 during Rosh Hashanah 2037-2038.

    1997   Leo begins
    + 40   Mirror reign
    2037   Ishmael ends

Will fire consume everything on earth like a burnt offering? If man survives, will he continue to fall short and repeat this whole process over again? Will God rest one thousand years after the Hebrew head of the year in 2037-2038? Will there be a new beginning similar to Noah's day? While we all recognize the story of Noah's Ark, we typically attribute less emphasis to the importance of God saving the animals and preservation of the whole earth. He washed it clean. Will God be consistent in saving some animals and regenerating the whole "earth" again? If a New Jerusalem comes down from heaven does that imply starting completely over? Since God's

Word is never-ending should that imply our current world is without end?

The year 2017 was also coined the year of the "Great American Eclipse." Some suggest that 2017 began a 7-year countdown toward 2024 simply because the darkness covered 7 cities named Salem. Salem means peace in Hebrew. This draws a direct connection to Jeru-salem which translates as the city of peace. Muslims attempt to mirror that context by translating the word Islam to mean peace in the Arabic tongue. In any regard, why would a solar eclipse carry any Biblical weight? Isn't this all purely conjecture or just words on a page? Answering this line of reasoning sufficiently may not be fully possible. However, there are a few items worth mentioning. There are references to a one-time unexplained eclipse recorded in 30 A.D. by historians Phlegon, Thallus, Africanus, and Tertullian as well as by Matthew, Mark, and Luke. This was unexplained in that it defied regularity of sequence and timing. In other words, eclipses occur at regular intervals, but this event was abnormal. Also abnormal was the duration of the effect. This eclipse lasted 3 hours. There has never been a case of such an occasion lasting more than 7-8 minutes. Therefore, this eclipse must be relevant at some level.

In the Old Testament darkness was eliminated in Genesis on the 4th day of creation. In the New Testament darkness was defeated by Christ on the cross. Here can be seen 2 occasions where darkness has been eradicated with a 3rd event arriving in Revelation. Earlier we discussed the Passover Festival as the 1st of 3 major feasts. It tells the story of how darkness Passes over the land to save the firstborn of God's creation. The 1st occasion occurred in Egypt for the Jews, and the 2nd event arrived in 30 A.D. for the Christians. The 2nd application concludes with Yeshua's death at 3 pm as the eclipse ends. Though the eclipse lasted 3 hours, Jesus spent 6 hours suffering while crucified on the cross. So, half of His time mounted on the cross was spent in darkness during the eclipse. This division of times by 2 is applicable throughout this book. Nearly the entire stage of the New Testament age is divided by representing the spiritual kingdom onset by the cross on one hand and the arrival of the Antichrist, religion, and false prophet on the other. Endeavoring to count any timelines such as these our key remains in Genesis. For example, creation days began at dusk and continued through the next day until sunset. Today, society tends to think that the morning starts the next day. These factors have caused great confusion when deciphering basic information such as when Christ was Crucified and rose from the dead. This becomes pertinent as it may also shed light on the times of His return. It may also become relevant that Passover in 30 A.D. did not fall on the traditional Saturday Sabbath. This was not usual. All 7 feasts or High Holy Sabbaths typically fall on varying weekdays from year to year.

The next chart lists each day through the resurrection with the supporting verses. The list shows a 3-hour eclipse ending with the death of Christ at 3 pm. Thursday required extra preparation for the coming High Holy Day of Passover that evening on Nissan 14. Friday evening started the Saturday Sabbath, the 7th day of Godly rest. Jesus would not rise on the 7th day of rest lest any man consider that working on the Sabbath. This book has consistently shown Jesus returns on the 8th day, Sunday. This theme was also demonstrated by the 50th Jubilee year, also known as the 8th Sabbatical year. The most agreeable part for Christians was that Jesus rose from the dead on a Sunday morning. Matthew 12 uses the story of Jonah in the belly of the beast to mirror how Jesus spent 3 days and 3 nights at the earth's core. This directly implicates where the beast currently resides, and that Yeshua was in captivity by the opposition. Whether or not Jesus was captive should no longer be of further debate. Just as Jonah came out of the beast's belly white from digestive juices, so too are we washed white as snow. Thankfully, Yeshua's payment for all of our sins is perpetual. Soon this wiley scapegoat will be permanently removed from this realm. That fallen alien will be eternally expelled, condemned by his own words only to be banished to Orion's lightless prison stronghold.

Days	Weekday	30 A.D. crucifixion events
-1-0	Wednesday	Last Supper
0-1	Thursday	Cross 9 am – 3 pm Noon – 3 pm eclipse Evening starts the next day
1-2	Friday	High Holy Day Passover John 18-19 Day before Sabbath
2-3	Saturday	Sabbath Saturday
3	Sunday	Risen Sunday morning before sunrise - 4 gospels

In recognition of Thursday's crucifixion, the Old Covenant Church temple gates began opening at 9 am documented as the 3rd hour of the day also dubbed as the 1st hour of prayer. The 2nd hour of prayer for the church became the 9th hour of the day at 3 pm. Though Revelation speaks of the temple gates opening, Jesus mentions a return during the night or morning hours. Without question, the final destruction will descend as a thief in the night upon His return for vengeance against the unbeliever. Although most churches suppose a rapture comes well before Armageddon. The question for us is… to which event does He refer?

A more cumbersome sign of Christ's return rests with analyzing Thursday's crucifixion eclipse. Clearly, there are astronomical implications. But, identifying all the complex dynamics in play is probably pointless for our purposes. Tackling the subject around the edges, we recognize that various eclipse cycles overlap. At some point, they all end, and new cycles begin. These cycles, called saros, arise from a harmonic between 3 of the moon's orbital cycles. Saros cycles occur approximately every 18 years. Each year these cycles produce varying degrees of darkness with varying frequency of events across the globe. Stephenson noted that one eclipse in 1406 was so dark that people believed the world was ending. Each eclipse viewpoint shifts geographically because the earth rotates an additional 120 degrees between each eclipse. During the next Saros cycle from October 2023 to October 2041, there will be 40 solar eclipses. NASA charts show Saros cycle #127 as having total eclipses in 2001, 2019, and 2037. Another red flare, Saros #127 contains 42 total and 42 partial eclipses. Notice that the numbers 40 and 42 are expressed during the same window of the projected return of Yeshua. Saros #136 includes other prescribed dates of 1973, 2009, and 2027. Interestingly, Saroses #127 and 136 add up to 10.

  1 + 2 + 7 = 10

  1 + 3 + 6 = 10

Each eclipse date corresponds to specific events. The total eclipse during 8/2/2027 will be visible from Jerusalem at 10:07 am which is 3:07 am on the east coast of the United

States. In addition, 2026, 2028, and 2030 each have 1 solar eclipse. Still another cycle, Saros #120 incorporates 1997, 2015, and 2033 as having total eclipses.

Here is a chart to help clarify this information:

Year	Solar 18yrs 11 days	Blood Moon - 19yr calendar
2025	2 Partial	2 Total - Jerusalem 9/7-8
2026	1 Annual 1 Total	2 T - J 8/27-28
2027	1 A 1 T - J 8/2	2 Penumbral 1 Almost
2028	1 A 1 T - leap year	2 Partial 1 T - J 12/31-1/1
2029	4 P	2 T - J 12/20-21
2030	1 A 1 T - J 6/1	1 P 1 Pe - 12/9-10
2031	1 Hybrid 1 A	3 Pe
2032	1 A 1 P - leap year	2 T - J 10/18-19, *Mercury*
2033	1 P 1 T	2 T - J 4/14-15
2034	1 A 1 T - J 3/20	1 P 1 Pe

197

2035	1 A 1 T	1 P 1 Pe
2036	3 P - leap year	2 T - J 2/11-12
2037	1 P 1 T	1 P 1 T Age ends 8th feast
2038	2 A 1 T - J 1/5, 7/2	4 Pe New Jerusalem

As stated, I don't pretend to know all the nuances of how God works all the numbers, I only know that He does. All God's forces work under a singular, orderly, mathematical framework. Not one jot or tittle exists without a precise measurement. For example, 99% of the human body is comprised of 6 elements: carbon, oxygen, hydrogen, nitrogen, calcium, and phosphorus. Carbon 12 has 6 protons, 6 electrons, and 6 neutrons. Thus,

The number of a man = 666

So, when I read 18 years between Saros cycles there exists singularity.

$6 + 6 + 6 = 18$

Then I read each eclipse viewpoint shifts geographically because the earth rotates an additional 120 degrees between each eclipse. And, why does Saros #120 have the only total eclipse in 1997? These were the numbers explored in Genesis when multiplied by 50, a Jubilee. Is this more coincidental hyperbole?

120 x 50 = 6,000 years

4004 B.C. - 6000 years = 1997 A.D.

Why wouldn't it also make sense that each eclipse might be a warning sign? Could the planet Mercury be sending us a message for the following year? Will communications be lost in the leap year of 2032? Is 2032 or 2033 the 2nd chance at a rapture event? As foretold, 2032 marks the end of the 1st term of 2 for the United Nations Secretary-General. Does the end of the Secretary-General's 2nd term signal 2037 as the end of the Age? Or are the 2 annual solar eclipses in 2038 enlightening us something further? The orbital diagram for 2038 on timeanddate.com shows 2 annual eclipses crossing each other twice within the Atlantic Ocean. Remarkably, both intersections appear to form a fish. The ocean or sea symbolizes the multitudes of people. These two lines forming a fish are the universal picture of Christianity. 1st century Christians would draw a curved line in the sand while the approaching traveler would draw the 2nd curved line forming a fish. These actions were a communication to believing strangers conveying friendship. Both eclipses in 2038 cover the land of Israel. Is this the final covering example like Sukkot? Does 2038 signal the onset of New Jerusalem?

Seemingly left out of the conversation is the year 2029. However, the arrangement of leap years, solar, and lunar eclipses, combined with our previous informational charts seem to point to this position. Stating the obvious, there are 2 types of eclipses, solar and lunar. Counting after the year, notice the 2nd column represents the lunar eclipses. Scroll down to the year 2029. It is scheduled for 4 partial solar eclipses and 2 total lunar eclipses. Now scroll back down to the last row again. Did you also pick up on the 4 lunar eclipses in 2038? Remember, the number 4 is the creation day that divided the day and night connecting the distance from heaven to earth. Are both (2) sets of 4 lunar eclipses pointing to significant events? The 2 total eclipses of 2029 seem incredibly timely. Only during a total lunar eclipse does the moon turn a reddish hue. Scripture refers to this hue color as "blood" in several places such as Joel 2 and Revelation 6. Under these circumstances, a blood moon becomes an immediate warning sign. Is this a warning for the following year, 2030?

Because of the layout of events, it seems less likely that a leap year will mark a return date. While Leap years help align lunar and solar cycles, the requirement of adding an extra day or month when comparing Judaic and Gregorian calendars could be perceived as problematic. Each Metonic cycle lasts approximately 19 years. You'll remember that Noah's lifespan was divided into 2 sets of 19. Perhaps one set denotes B.C., and the other A.D. Leap years occur every 4 years except for years divisible by 100 but not by 400. Therefore, I am ruling out 2028, 2032, and 2036. In review, 30 A.D. was not a leap, nor is 2030. This redirects the emphasis on 2029-2030 or before if one believes in a rapture before 2037. Of course, this only scratches the surface and doesn't prove anything definitive without other supporting information. But it does build confidence knowing that God is in complete control from start to finish. Yet, this in no way prescribes to the god of numerology but rather the God of creation which is order beyond all comprehension.

Yet, there lingers an underlying question asked that must be sought after. Did the sun truly stand still for 3 hours while Christ remained nailed on the cross? In Joshua chapter 10 God extends the light long enough to ensure a victorious battle for the chosen ones. According to Fernand Crombette ancient Egyptian hieroglyphics tell a story of Joshua's long day. Greek historian Herodotus writes of the same story after visiting Egyptian priests. Mayan and Peruvian Indians tell the same story. Various North American Indian tribes also report these stories. Eyewitness accounts verify these events did happen. God altered either the moon's orbit, the earth's orbit, or both (2) in each instance. Perhaps this caused an earthquake as recorded in 30 A.D.

Will a nuclear war cause earthquakes? Just north of Jerusalem lies an area marked for eruption. There are many such areas across the globe. The obvious regions of concern are comprised of ongoing volcanic activity. The United States has one of the world's largest dormant calderas located in Yellowstone National Park. Underground signs have increasingly suggested that activity is underway. An eruption of this scale would wipe out crops across North America. Volcanic ash would block out the sun and decrease world temperatures. The sun and moon would appear as blood. Will God freeze these proceedings just before an eruption, and remove His elect? Consider that Joshua would go on to fight the Canaanites for 7 years. Can we also expect to endure 7 more years of war after a major eruption or battle? Was 2023 the beginning of Israel's 7 years of war like Joshua entering the Promised Land? Should we draw similarities to Ezekiel 43 when considering our hope to be spared? Ezekiel 43 ends with God accepting the Hebrews on the 8th day, after 7 days of burnt offerings. We can conclude this proposes deliverance after war and repentance. Is this another indication of a 2nd opportunity for covering the converting Messianic Jew? Is one of these impending events the world's 3rd and final example of a day that time stands still?

LOVE AND IDEOLOGY

Society's assessment of love surreptitiously varies from individual to individual. The word has become so casually engaged that it rarely carries the weight it was initially intended to bear. If we enjoy ice cream the phrase is overly used to describe the gravity of how much we "love" it. Additionally, words can be imprecise, and our norms can often bring about incorrect practices that, over time, become acceptable usages of terms and phrases. Sometimes this lingo spills over into societal norms. For example, if we say "love is love" then, culture argues that love should apply no matter the context. However, all contexts have boundaries. Instinctively, everyone knows that if no boundaries existed then, nothing could ever be consistently defined. Everything would become forever fluid and meaningless. Like it or not, all boundaries are outlined by our level of faith. For example, if a culture agrees that anyone can marry whomever they please, that belief directly opposes scripture. Thus, the more separated one's religious beliefs operate outside of politics the less understanding one likely possesses of scripture. A common misconception states that a civilization must separate itself from religion in order to operate at the highest level. Yet, without an ethical culture laws begin to defy morality. Furthermore, if we claim a man can become a woman, or vice versa, simply out of one's desire then we deny science, reason, and morality. When this becomes the case, our political ideology becomes our god. This ideology takes root when a void of prayer is present. Many citizens never stop to consider prayer before casting their vote. Perhaps if we admitted this ideology usurped our faith, would we be required to change the vote? Or worse, our ideology. Thus, we are implying that our political ideology will save us or that we know better than God. "I got this." Bluntly, are we placing our trust in the candidate or the Creator?

Must God have the monopoly on defining love? To what God must we all prescribe? If we cannot answer both questions accurately, it signals our barometer level of belief. If a culture cannot adequately come to grips with the fact that God is love and that He alone defines intimacy, then no love can ever be fully extended to others. That love source will be trapped, turned inward feeding upon itself. Acts of intimacy become empty, selfish, and underwhelming. Anyone desiring fulfillment should ask if anyone can truly love when they do not know the love giver. Furthermore, can we be saved at all without love? God saves the person who searches for the Truth with a pure heart. That decision to worship a God or not to devote oneself seems to be a recurring opinion. Most people professing a belief in a higher power prefer to be comforted by thinking they have an earthly choice in the matter. Regardless, after that initial commitment many tend to waver, often lacking desire beyond simply entering those pearly gates. These decisions spill over into our daily lives in the most basic way, to love one another.

Yet, it is also a safe assumption that we cannot fully love without freedom. The belief in personal freedom and a higher power collide with the formation of governments. History paints many empires as having evil antichrist-like traits. In our day, Marxism corresponds to the last season of empires. In this vain, it is logical to inquire if a socialist can love God or anyone else for that matter. Of course, this very idea of excluding someone based on their ideology would be considered highly offensive, particularly to a socialist. Nevertheless, this typical response envelopes the nature of the mentality of a socialist. It is the red flag that searches for an accuser in which to blame their victimhood. Such outward aggression shows a psychological transference, a common symptom of inwardly suppressed love. That trapped love manifests outwardly in the form of hate and destruction. Hoarding love often results in vindictive behavior toward others. Thus, an individual's moral compass is directly tied to how we treat others which can only be attributed to a right-standing relationship with God. Depriving ourselves of God's love pushes us against all of civilization around us. If that is the case, and it is, where do we go from here? We can go nowhere apart from prayer. And, if that is true, and it is, why is it that so many professing to love others rarely pray at all? Does a nightly 1 minute "Our Father" prayer meet the threshold of a relationship? Can a couple maintain a marriage based on 10 minutes a day of discussion? Does an hour a week for church service represent a relationship or a tithe?

It is amazing how individuals trap themselves inside their thought processes. Their minds are a maze of snares and crippling thoughts driving them away from acts of freedom such as prayer. Sadly, prayer is a hidden secret of modern religion tucked away as if unimportant to a vast majority of professing Christians. Do not misunderstand, Christians will confess to the importance of prayer at least to some degree and might even participate in reciting the Lord's prayer but there is no real commitment to knowing God. When prayer is sidestepped, personal responsibility is absent. Knowing ourselves better becomes comfortably avoidable. There exists no serious commitment to correcting deeply held habits. Therefore, intimate discipline is lacking because devotion is halfhearted at best. Our effectiveness and fulfillment as Christians are diminished. Intercessory prayers are virtually nonexistent. This is key to helping others. Ironically, intercessory prayers aid in healing ourselves. Yet, God allows us some freedom to do or not to do what is right and healthy for our own existence. God does not force us to love. But make no mistake, those who refuse to love according to scripture will not enter into rest. He provides all the good things we lack if we ask according to His Word. Yahweh can even become the Father to the fatherless.

Because Yahweh voluntarily takes up our slack whenever we fall short, there can be no excuse for failure. We need only to let go and ask. Judgment comes upon everyone not covered by the blood of the Lamb. The fairest way to administer judgment is to allow people to judge themselves, although the Truth compels us to speak the Word. All creation is compelled as a witness for the Truth. Romans 8 says the whole world groans the closer we come to Yeshua's return. These Truths have always been self-evident. When Christ removes those who subscribe to justice the Holy Spirit will no longer restrain evil for a short span. People will be left to their own devices for solutions. They will finally be granted the chance to rule without Godly intervention. This is the opportunity sought after since the foundations of the world for everyone who denies the deity of Yahweh. This will be fair to both (2) parties, those who follow true order and those who follow the "New Order" of chaos. All under that code will witness total collapse.

Unconditional love and forgiveness will be absent because, without repentance, there can be no genuine forgiveness. When there is no forgiveness, love becomes conditional. Neither, can self-prescribed victims legitimately subscribe to love; only their evil can be reciprocated. Make no mistake, God is no respecter of persons. He is faithful to administer justice under the law equally. Now we can see how God disburses final judgment and how it is in effect self-imposed. Exercising this freedom to abandon the Truth dooms us to separation from the love of God, which provides forgiveness through His mercy and grace. Jesus was "cut off" for our transgressions but we must acknowledge the Truth. To be "cut off" inside the lake of fire is merely a result that each individual freely chooses. It is not what a loving God wishes on anyone. A short-sighted view conveniently leaves these facts unexplored. Or worse, they blame God for their own shortcomings. If they pray, their prayers arrive after judgment and miss the will of God. We hide these snares inside our daily lives like dynamite used to blow up any good reason to worship an angry God.

Prayers and praise are recorded as sweet incense before the Lord, Psalms 141. Yet, might there be a more revealing back story about prayers? Could it be that our prayers and praise are supposed to have replaced those fallen angels that now obstruct us? Is that why God has made us priests, Revelation 1? Will that be our heavenly position as sons of the Living God? 1/3 of the Heavenly Hosts fell with the angel in charge of worship. 1/3 of the angels remain under Michael's command for battle and 1/3 are messengers under Gabriel. With this knowledge, we understand that God preserved spiritual purity by maintaining sovereignty. The world tells us the fight is Physical. Jesus prays and fasts showing us the battle is spiritual. The last spiritual battle Jesus tells us might actually have been foreshadowing the coming antichrist. It may not be obvious at first glance.

Biblestudytools.com gives terrific background information regarding why Jesus wants His disciples to meet Him in Galilee after the resurrection in Matthew 26. Jesus returns to the place where it all started just as Moses had claimed the land centuries beforehand. This area marked ground zero for the gospel ministry. The "Jesus Revolution" was to begin here. Jesus and the disciples were all considered Galileans, Acts 13. Yeshua's 1st miracle in John 2 was when all the disciples first believed. Matthew 4 describes Galilee as "The Way...to the sea" and says the people there lived in darkness. Kedesh was a city situated in those hills on the way to the sea. Kedesh seemingly mocked Matthew 5 as if they existed in the light of knowledge. The area was divided into 2 regions, paganism and the fallen tribe of Dan. Kedesh has a long history of gentile paganism and is strikingly similar to Ishamel's city of Kadesh located further south. 1 Kings 9 calls the area Cabul - "like nothing" but a more correct meaning is circle or revolution. The Rock Revolution would clash against Ishmael and all paganism, smashing the antichrist into pieces like clay vessels. How can anyone avoid this fate? The Bible says to come out of her. Prayer redeems our Fatherly relationship by reestablishing a conversation, a connection.

When is it too late to be redeemed by the Rock of salvation? That day is referenced in several books such as Proverbs 29.

What is prayer anyway? Can anyone clearly define prayer? Prayer is talking with God, rather than to God. This initiates a deeper personal relationship with the Father. Without this consistent disciplinary action, we cannot become our best mature creation. The action of prayer accelerates the renewal process by replacing our old habits with Godly habits. Without it, we limp along living a mostly unfulfilled lifestyle that often resembles trying to will ourselves into the right relationship by following a set of dos and don'ts. Such individual effort will result in either doing nothing or accomplishing very little. Only after the power of the Holy Spirit is granted living dominion within us can there be consistently true freedom and comfort, John 14:16-18. It boils down to 2 options; live by our decisions in constant distress or choose His direction living in peace and freedom, 2 Corinthians 3:17.

Prayer is a continuation of the humble renewing of the mind beginning with a confession of faith through acceptance of the Son. This opens the door to free reign by the Holy Spirit. The Holy Spirit reveals the Father's plan, Romans 12:2. Our Father only listens to the committed believer, John 9:31. Every faithful believer is worthy of God's attention. No experience is necessary. In this Way, prayer is available to everyone, 1 Corinthians. No one begins the journey as a spiritual giant and no one ever "arrives," Acts 10:34-35. Prayer is not feelings-based, but timely obedience. Listening to God's voice allows us to pray as the Spirit directs, John 5:19. Even still, we are active participants, not bystanders. Exercising this discipline gains insight into events and prophetic perspectives.

You might ask, how do I even begin this process? What is required? First, let's visit three reasons why most people never take prayer seriously. They should sound familiar.

1. They don't truly wish to devote themselves to Christianity as a disciple.

2. They are lazy, at least until a crisis arises.

3. They don't really want to change themselves.

1st, inward examination comes through self-reflection, which is prayer, Psalm 139: 23-24. This requires constant attitude adjustments. A lack of humility will not permit prayer or any specific repentance. By specific repentance, I mean to say that some may admit to not being perfect though never pinning down anything specific that needs self-addressing. This begs the 2nd point, have they truly decided to follow a faithful Savior or not, Matthew 13:4-9. When there is no calling to faith, there is no prayer, no fruit. 3rd, faith is exhibited by our level of discipline weaved into our continual daily commitment to prayer, 1 Thessalonians 5:17-18. If we elect not to pray, there are consequences beyond ourselves, 2 Chronicles 7:14. On the other hand, when we pray, God grants us peace, Philippians 4:6-7. Let us practice a prayer together: "Father, thank you for listening. Please help me address my disobedience, lack of humility, and lack of understanding. I do not want to continue walking away from You. So, I ask You to make repentance a reality in my heart. Give me Your grace, and a desire to pray. Lord, increase my faith to pray according to Your will. All praise and honor to You, O' LORD. ICN, Amen.

Here are some options to help you get started. Some may begin praying by meditating on a particular verse or situation, Psalm 119:15 & 97. Others may try playing soft worship or praise music when nothing specific is on their mind, Psalm 100:2. As this becomes a soaking prayer, you will eventually prefer quiet to hear God's voice, John 10:4. At first, I imagined being prostrate at the feet of God. It grounded me to focus solely on Him. Later that was supplemented by experiencing His presence, Psalm 139. Worship can also touch spirit to spirit, God's with ours. The benefits of prayer produce inward and outward healing. Often this is not understood or even recognizable at first glance. I recommend starting with a goal of 15 minutes. It will lengthen over time, effortlessly. At some point, you will achieve daily perpetual communion.

So far, soaking prayer consists of active listening or meditation, confession, worship, praise, and petition. Soaking prayer is not "Flash Prayer." Quick prayers address daily concerns, such as when children cry or if someone requests a passing need. These are important requests that intercede on behalf of others. But this does not supplant soaking prayer in the presence of God. This is the beginning of effective intercessory prayer. Intercessory prayers display compassion, love, mercy, etc. These are faith-building opportunities in our walk, 1 Timothy 2. Intercessory prayer drives believers deeper into scripture and the maturation process called discipleship. In turn, this re-enforces another prayer cycle and a new level of spiritual awareness, 2 Timothy 3:12-17. Never forget, Jesus is our saving intercessor, John 15-21. We are participants in His will, not dictators.

How do fasting and prayer work together? Am I required to fast? First, consider if there are any health issues. Medical clearance may need to be considered. Some may choose a Daniel fast/diet. Some may mention there is no commandment to fast. Yet, one of the first things Jesus did was to go into the wilderness and pray. Upon His return, the scripture points out that the Apostles had difficulty casting out a particular demon that required fasting and prayer, Matthew 17. So, fasting and prayer must be important. In addition, it speeds up the maturation process when the fast focuses on God and not the food sacrifice. Consequently, fasting means feasting only on the Word of God. Consider testing yourself to a fast of 12 hours, try midnight to noon, or sunset to sundown. Expand it to 1 special holiday or agreement between you and God. Fasting seems to be an action capable of bringing the body and mind under the subjection of the soul/spirit, a symbol of 3 in 1.

The final question is why join a group to pray? Why can't I pray at home? Of course, and you should. However, unity in prayer multiplies the effectiveness. Here are a few other reasons.

1. An organized group of like-minded disciples will strengthen and accelerate your effectiveness for God.

2. It makes us accountable.

3. It allows us to participate in God's anointing power of healing.
4. Standing in the gap for the afflicted reflects God's character of love and mercy.

5. Those freed from bondage also have great power against those same demons to deliver others.

Here are the top four fence sitter responses:

1. Why me? If you are called to intercede, you are worthy. No experience necessary.

2. What if I am new to this whole idea? Experience with religion can sometimes be a hindrance. New believers possess pure firepower that only needs direction and protection.

3. Will I see any results or verifiable miracles? Getting involved dramatically increases those chances. When you get involved God will work miracles in your life and others.

4. What should I expect? Expect to see God work miracles and all sorts of healings. Some

immediately, some gradually. As you begin making an impact expect the enemy to make an entrance. Resist and the devil will flee, James 4:7. For this reason, intercessors should pray for one another first.

The battle is against principalities and powers of darkness, Colossians 1:16, Daniel 10:20, Isaiah 24:21. Will we fight that battle or succumb by ignorance, Hosea 4:6? These are the choices freedom brings. How we view these choices is merely the tricks and trappings we place upon ourselves to alleviate our conviction of laziness. We implore these snares to relax in our idleness. For example, one excuse that has become more common lately is insomnia or the report of a lack of sleep in general. Expect this type of report to become more widespread as we approach the end of this age. Here's an interesting perspective, have you ever considered that it might be the Lord attempting to get our attention during these quiet morning hours? Could time be almost running out? The point has been made clear. God calls everyone to pray. And, God wants us to pray for each other. Without prayer, faith becomes our handy work and is dead.

Some Christians profess to have unlocked knowing the will of God through prayer. However, if one splices any verses out of context to arrive at a formula-based prayer technique professing to heal all who have enough faith it cannot be scriptural. The obvious proof rests with 2 well-known stories. Paul prayed for his affliction 3 times with no relief. Surely Paul had faith but was never healed. Secondly, Jesus prayed for God to pass the cup of the cross that lay before Him. Yet, Jesus submitted to the will of the Father knowing the outcome. There was no other Way. Isn't it interesting that Jesus prayed without getting His way? Likewise, neither did Paul get relief. Paul's affliction kept him subservient to God's purpose in his life. More is at play in our lives than assuming God has planned that everyone will be healed. Faith is certainly an important component, but it is not the only ingredient. Daily prayer delivers that spiritual connection to know the direction God has for living our lives. Then we can pray with confidence knowing God hears us and we hear Him. Sometimes our predestined lives require other things from us to carry out God's purpose. Who else knows how to bring forth good works than the Spirit who works through us and in us, Philippians 2?

A friend's daughter began singing in the church band recently. He shared that after her latest Sunday service, she mentioned to him how touched she was when noticing some of the people in the congregation began crying during song worship. The people's response to her singing became an encouragement to her God-given gifts. This is how God often works. He blesses those who use their gifts in service to Him. God seeks a pure heart, not a perfect person. The young singer was serving out of joy for God, not for the results. Noah got no positive responses except from his own family. God blessed Noah and the singer with unforeseen fruits. Intercessory prayer works very similarly. Though the results of our prayers often go unseen in the natural sense they have an impact beyond this realm, reaching into eternity. So, even though we may not be pastoring a church, the Scripture says we are priests in His church body. If we are not actively praying and sharing, we cheat God, the body of Christ, and ourselves out of the fruit of the spirit. We cheat ourselves out of love, joy, peace, patience, kindness, goodness, faithfulness, and gentleness.

ILLUSIONS AND ILLUSTRATIONS

The beginning chapters of this book suggested a staging ground for participants within the confines of a universal set of laws such as space, gravity, and time. These parameters were set forth as an hourglass to encase a finite period that would end projecting the Truth of God's Sovereign Word. In so doing, the creation of time was born as interpreted by these laws in which we currently exist. Keep in mind, that if man was created with no imperfections, he must have at least initially been immortal. So, it may also be a reasonable assumption that time did not exist within the boundaries of the Garden. Nevertheless, for us, time is an illusion of creation that will cease to exist when the witness of this age has been completed. Quantum entanglement seems to be finally embracing my concept of this illusion, a departure from the long-standing fundamental aspect.

According to quantum entanglement, objects appear static to external observers, like a painting rather than a timeline. Scientists surmise that a reference clock controls this fabric regardless of distance. However, scientists have yet to admit the realization that the reference clock is positioned outside of our universe of laws. Once experts link the previously discovered sound wave source emitting from outside this universe to quantum entanglement, new questions must be faced. Then, we can surmise that heaven exists outside this speck we call a universe. This idea has been ignored because it was thought to challenge Einstein's views shaped by general relativity for the past 100 years. On the contrary, quantum entanglement may unify mathematics.
Researchers Alessandro Coppo and colleagues published their findings in *__Physical Review A.__*

> "For centuries, time has entered physics as an essential ingredient that is not to be questioned. It is so deeply rooted in our conception of reality that people thought that a definition of time was not needed…" "We believe that nature is genuinely quantum…"

The implications suggest a bridging of the gap between quantum mechanics and general relativity. Reconciling these 2 perspectives requires a rethinking of time and singularity. This idea of singularity will likely collide with Ai. Kurzweil theorized that artificial general intelligence would occur in 2029 over twenty years ago. Once humans and machines become integrated the corruption described as in the day of Noah's Nephilim will be completed. The promises of intellectual freedom will turn into a chaotic reality. The artificial world of Ai will bring destruction. This time fire will rain down instead of water all the while waving a diversified flag picturing a rainbow. On this day, fabrication theory will meet reality.

Sometimes people pay attention to science; sometimes people prefer statistics; sometimes they hide behind a thin veneer mixed with clay, and sometimes they do not hide at all. Eventually, the simple Truth of God's covenants should be recognizable within the festivals. These truths should shed light on the importance of these feasts as they testify to the events that everyone should have known to be present. Nonetheless, the Bible features several key covenants between God and humanity. Except for the first agreement God's covenants present a summary of redeeming humanity. A covenant is a binding relationship between two partners who make promises to each other to reach a common goal. In the scriptures, we see accompanying oaths and ceremonies within the festivals, etcetera. Jesus has already fulfilled the signs of the first 4 festivals. The last 4 festivals lead us to the covenant of marriage with Christ. Though some suggest a list of ten, here are 8 covenants:

Starting in Genesis the Edenic Covenant included blessings and a command not to eat from the Tree of Knowledge of good and evil. Once this warning went unheeded, Adam and Eve were spiritually locked out of heaven and driven out of the garden. Thus, the Adamic covenant was a result of disharmony and death. Death evolves as Cain murders his brother. Interestingly, in Genesis 5 this topic of "died" is repeated 8 times. Here we see the seals displayed should we decidedly acknowledge the evil accelerating by the time of the Noahic Covenant. God restores creation after washing the world and saving a remnant aboard the Ark. The rainbow signifies God's promise never to repeat that scenario. From this juncture, it becomes an abomination to substitute a rainbow for any other action or cause.

4th is the Abrahamic Covenant. God promised Abraham many descendants and retained Israel as His chosen people. This remains true in the New Testament despite the attitude of many leader's insistence to the contrary. Romans 11 states this truth 3 times. It should be noted that remaining God's chosen people doesn't mean that Jewish people have forgiveness and a personal relationship with God. Even Jewish people must learn to trust Jesus as the Messiah for salvation. Therefore, most of the seed of Abraham is likely spread worldwide sprinkled in various denominations that espouse Jesus Christ as Lord. The Abrahamic covenant is also accompanied by an outward sign liken to the rainbow. Once a male child is 8 years old, he is to be circumcised. Here again is another reference to the 8th day. Islam does not recognize circumcision but instead receives judgment in the 8th year. Now we see the scripture unfolding as the 8th day is also when Jesus rose from the dead. This is likely the year of our marriage to Christ.

5th is the Mosaic Covenant given to Moses on Mount Sinai. Remember there were 2 trips separated by 10 days, 2 tablets with 5 commandments each. Herein are hidden 3 sets of 5 denoting Christ's free grace. Rather than receiving that gift, the Israelites chose a golden calf. As a result, the judgment produced 3,000 slain. Is it possible that the 3,000 was determined within the story details?

5	Commandments
x 5	Commandments
x 2	Tablets
x 3	Sets of 5
x 2	Trips
x 10	Days
3000	Slain

While this could be a stretch, it makes a point. If the Jews chose not to observe Yahweh and the Sabbath, more would fall into destruction. Christians would be wise to take heed. The 6th Priestly Covenant was to ensure the path of righteousness. The Levites were a chosen tribe within the chosen people mirroring the 8th. Keep in mind the 6th was considered stripped from priesthood before the arrival of Yeshua. The 7th Davidic Covenant promised King David his descendants would rule Israel forever, concluding with the Messiah as ordained in 2 Samuel 7. The 8th Covenant brings us into the New Testament completing the redemption story as expressed in Luke 22. Thus, the New Covenant established through the Messiah of David's lineage would restore all things and be everlasting. This proves God's Kingdom was fulfilled with Christ and has no end.

Mathew 25 tells the parallel story of 10 virgins, 5 were foolish and 5 were prudent. The wise disciples exercised their faithfulness daily and were seen fit to be "caught up" upon the Lord's return. Those virgin priests walked by the spiritual promises made by God and not by sight. So, here we surmise the opposite of faith is not doubt but living by sight which produces doubt. Those living by any other avenues will endure forever but void of those luxuries offered through God's promises of peace, love, etc. Although, some would submit the story continues for 2 additional covenants. Depending on one's perspective this might include the elect's marriage to the Lamb and the emergence of New Jerusalem. There is little doubt, God's 3rd temple will be constructed with the advent of New Jerusalem to house this ceremony. In any case, our focus remains fixed upon the event that befalls society before New Jerusalem. In that light, let us revisit several keys previously mentioned that might intertwine with the 8 covenants listed.

Expounding upon the story of Jacob and his first 2 brides, he works the first 7 years only to find his marriage was to Leah rather than Rachel. Consequently, Jacob works a 2nd stint of 7 years to marry his intended bride, Rachel. After the 14th year of servitude to his father-in-law, Jacob finally marries his first love. This similar numerical pattern was reiterated in the story of Abraham, Hagar, and Sara. Abraham is 100 and Ishmael is 14 when Isaac was born by Sarah. As established, the true cyclical Sabbatical year fell in September 2023. By extrapolating both stories one could surmise that 2 windows of opportunity exist. The 1st window opens between 2023-2030 and the 2nd window might open between 2031-2038. The story seems to be confirmation that the chosen are caught up in the 1st 7-year cycle and the uncircumcised Ishmaelites are left for judgment after the 2nd 7-year cycle concludes. This also falls within the parameters of King David and King Solomon's reign in the Old Testament. God was faithful to Israel by permitting both kings to reign for 40 years. Notice how both periods sync with Israel's rebirth.

    1948   Israel nationhood
    + 40   David's reign
    1988   Presidential prophecy

    1988   1st term ends
    + 40   Solomon's reign
    2028   2nd term ends

Interestingly, Genesis 25 tells us that Isaac marries Rebekah when he is 40. Each instance flashes a message that marriage signs are soon arriving on the horizon. Each flash of information reinforces the message of a narrowing window signaling Yeshua's impending return. We know from scripture that after King Solomon's death, Israel broke in 2. 10 Tribes remained in the north and 2 in the south. Both warred against each other. Regardless of any current possible peace negotiations regarding the 2023 Hamas invasion of Israel, we should expect additional conflict to break loose in Israel after the mirror of Solomon's reign in 2028-2030. Scripturally, this widening conflict will primarily include 10 participants.

Understanding that Israel mainly relies upon Big Brother United States we might suppose the presidential election bears importance. Currently, the media casts 2 presidential choices between totalitarian joy wrapped with frogs (see Revelation Made EZ) and free enterprise presented as greed and potential dictatorship. These 4 years linking Yom Kippur and Sukkot are designated to be distributed specifically by YHWH as shown in the next chapter. This cycle will likely be the last election as defined by natural law and unalienable rights under the United States Constitution. These 4 years represent several factors that will not be discussed fully yet coincide with the last 4 feasts. The trigger for these divinely designated years began with the designation of Jerusalem as the capital of Israel in 2017. By proclaiming this, President #45 paved the way for the final 20 years until the breakthrough occurs in 2037.

    2028   Solomon's reign ends
    + 10   Mirror Pentecost & Y = 10
    2038   Breakthrough age

According to Abarim Publications YHWH means, He Who Causes That-Which-Is To Be & He Who Causes That-Which-Can't-Be To Fall. From this we can understand that God is the Truth, the Way, the Creator of everything in this universe and heaven. Others say YHWH means "**I AM WHO I AM**" or "**I WILL BE WHAT I WILL BE.**" God's name has often been considered incomprehensible if for no other reason than because God is infinitely beyond any human words used to describe Him. While some religions claim to profess His name, they unknowingly use some definable derivative. Thankfully, God judges the heart while His grace remains sufficient for the meek. He is forever, I AM. Take care to read the calculation of YHWH = breakthrough:

Y = 10. It is the first 2-digit number = Father & Son. It is the fundamental building block for all Creation = the Word. 10 represents sanctity, holiness, priestly. The number 10 seems to be a benchmark when gathered in His name to overcome adversity. 10 spies scouting the land gave a poor report; 2 of the 12 spies scouting out the land gave good reports. 5 of the 10 virgins were of good report. Lot's city was burned because there were not 10 in good report.

1. There are the 10 Utterances of Speech through which God created the world.
2. Adam to Noah = 10 generations.
3. Noah to Abraham = 10 generations.
4. The Egyptian people were cursed with 10 plagues.
5. God performed 10 miracles saving His people.
6. 10 tests for the Jewish people in the desert.
7. God gives the 10 Commandments.

H = 5 represents grace for the soul. Each soul is tasked to unify 3 components; thought, speech, and action. 3 symbolizes the Christ. In this regard, we are all created equal under God, and all one. 5 represents the spark of redemption that ignites the seed of faith. There can be no initial action except by God to wake our seed by faith of revelation. Then, only by prayer can we find guidance lest we perform the labor from our own hands. Only 5 virgins had oil on that faithful day.
1. 2 levels of thought: imaginative, meditative
2. 2 levels of speech: the heart and lips
3. 1 level of action that displays faith or inaction

W = 6 binds what is in heaven and earth. Jewish scribes wrote the Torah in columns of 42 lines. Each scroll consisted of approximately 50 sheets. The 2nd Adam returns to take His oil home. Is this the 2nd chance for Hebrews? What about the 2nd letter H?

1. Man was created on day 6
2. Man works for 6 days
3. Mankind ends with 6 millennian
4. The Antichrist mirrors 3-6's, WWW, and 42
5. YHW + Jubilee = 1st rapture by 2nd Adam

(H) = The 2nd 5 extends grace for another day. It could extend a 2nd offering to Hebrews but 5 also may represent the books of Moses or the law.

After these 4 years, His Spirit will be removed from the land. Chaos will have free reign until those who remain are no more. These are the godless, selfish, egos quick to blame others when diving into the deep end of a pool. They sell the lie that they're not all wet. Yet, their emperor has no clothes, and the day is coming when every tongue will confess the facts. They knew or they should have known. Those who knew should have shouted from the mountaintops, but they kept quiet because of their positions.

Halfway through the next U.S. presidential term will bring us to Rosh Hashanah 2028, likely the 1st open window of opportunity. Thankfully, the New Covenant of grace is no respecter of persons. It is the completion of God's plan; one plan, one bible. Noticeably, Britain and the United States have played a major role in these plans. England begot the colonies, and both became world powers by putting the God of Abraham, Isaac, and Jacob first. Not commonly known is the word Brit means covenant, and the word Ish means man, "covenant with man." So, we can visually see the intentionality of Britian's birthright. Likewise, the United States was founded on Judeo-Christian values. Both countries were brothers bound to promote Israel's nationhood in 1948. The United States will stand until God's hand is removed. God's hand will be removed after the 1st 5 virgins are "caught up."

 2023 Jubilee
 + 5 5 virgins
 2028 Rapture window

After those with oil are removed, Jericho will collapse just as the bridge collapsed in Maryland. This was a picture of an impending omen unnoticed by the proud. Many are under the impression that a great falling away must occur first. However, several events in history already qualify. The more recent church apostasies omit God as the receiver of all prayers and embrace same-sex marriage. Perhaps the most forgotten falling away was the Concordat between Hitler and Pope Pius the 12th. In effect, it politicized the Catholic Church thereby neutering it and even making it complicit within Nazi Germany. The United States invasion of Italy spared the Catholic Church before the false prophet could destroy the Vatican. In the meantime, Hitler redefined Christianity in his own perverted image.

 1290 Daniel 12
 + 688 Abomination mosque
 1978 Camp David Accords

Remember, 1978 was a peace treaty with Palestine. Examine the dynamics when applied to the 3rd letter W in YHWH.

 1978 Camp David Accords
 + 50 Jubilee of 50 sheets
 2028 2nd Adam locks out 42

Extrapolating this circumstance W means the 2nd Adam binds the 42nd Ishmael on the 50th year of 2028. But what about the 2nd letter H? If the Antichrist is bound in 2028, Yom Kippur of 2029 may rescue the repentant Hebrew 1 year and 10 days later. Finally, both are rapture-type events will the elect be "caught up" alive or martyrs under the alter? Must we account for the dead in Christ to rise first, I Thessalonians 4:16?

JUST THE ESSENTIALS

<u>Seer in the Way</u> mentions a morning when a sense of dread came over me early in 2023. Once again, I did not know exactly what it meant, I just knew something pivotal had happened. One year later while in prayer the ground began shaking. It was slight but my curiosity was aroused. I inquired as to the cause, but all was silent. Yet, I was left with expectancy as if the answer would be shortly forthcoming. Nothing like this had happened to me before. The next week plus 1 day (8), the ground began to shake again. This time the quake lasted two days and carried more intensity. At the time I hoped it meant revival was coming. I did not perceive both quakes as separate events, though they would later be revealed as politically related. The following week another quake happened though it lingered a while on this 3rd cycle. It stopped on 7/13/2024, the day of the assignation attempt on President #45. On 7/21/2024, 8 days later president #46 resigned from his campaign seeking reelection. Bret Baier of Fox News reported this resignation as an earthquake event. That was the moment it all became clear. After that statement, it was easy to connect the dots. All these events are tied together to the very length of days.

This led me to ponder, does 2023 mark the beginning of the end? Are these the last 7 years the church believes as the end time tribulation? Feasibly, we should make one last review of all this material, visions, etcetera, and summarize how much time is most likely left. Taking a level-headed approach, it is reasonable to weigh all the evidence if for no other reason than simply narrowing the window of possibilities. Surely, we can reasonably surmise the season as the scripture says. If not, we must consider that Christians risk a similar error as the Jews omitting the Messiah's birth. This time, will there be 2nd group of Magi awaiting His return?

Nostradamus was a 16th-century French seer best known for his book Les Propheties. Having read some of his notes I believe Nostradamus was a devout Christian. And, while I do not profess to have studied all his works at least 2 prophecies have material contributions. Both are universally believed to reference the final antichrist. The first is commonly interpreted as he will wear a blue helmet or turban coming in the name of peace. As you read the following 7 resolutions or changes from the United Nations Security Council charter, ask yourself if this sounds like a peacekeeping force:

Article 41:

The Security Council may decide what measures not involving the use of armed force are to be employed to give effect to its decisions, and it may call upon the Members of the United Nations to apply such measures. These may include complete or partial interruption of economic relations of rail, sea, air, postal, telegraphic, radio, and other means of communication, and the severance of diplomatic relations.

Article 42:

Should the Security Council consider that measures provided for in Article 41 would be inadequate or have proved to be inadequate, it may take such action by air, sea, or land forces as may be necessary to maintain or restore international peace and security. Such action may include demonstrations, blockade, and other operations by air, sea, or land forces of Members of the United Nations.

Let's restate the Zoroastrian/economic agreement of the United Nations that is designed to supersede all government sovereignty in mathematical terms and see where that leads:

    2015 UN agreement
    + 14 2-week window
    2029 Event

Or/and

    2024 Jubilee
    + 14 2-week window
    2038 New Jerusalem

Secondly, and relatively recently, I received an email asking for the meaning of Nostradamus's quatrain MABUSH. This revelation was given to me before 2009. Here is the meaning of that mystery revealed to me more than 14 years ago. MABUSH is a combination of 2 last names of key people in reverse order. Both names are United States presidents who reigned after 1988, the first prophecy year already documented in my book series.

    1989 Election #41 Bush
    + 20 42 & 43
    2009 Halfway

    2009 Election #44 MA
    + 20 45, 46, 47
    2029 40-year reign ends

The first division (2) of 40 years began with the Bush family and the second half with Obama. Much discussion could be expounded upon about the CIA, the Patriot Act, and the Bush family but that is not the crux of our position. The 1st 20 years set the stage for Ishmael. According to the calculation, Obama will run the Socialist Democratic Party until 2029. From this understanding, Nostradamus's MABUSH mirrors the same consistency as Daniel's empires, except that Nostradamus is limited to 2 kings within 1 specific empire. Notwithstanding, Nostradamus did prophesy about other nations and kings which is not our current objective. Our objective explores a connection within the fabric of the United States of America. When we explore the birth of the United States 2 dates stand out above the rest, Independence Day and the adoption of the Constitution. The Constitution was ratified in 1787, and the Declaration of Independence was celebrated in 1776. Exactly 5 Jubilees from the ratification date land in 2037, already highlighted as the last season of this Age. Follow closely along with the second calculation. The date of U.S. independence until its' sovereignty ends is 239 years. That authority appears to be officially passed on to the U.N. in 2015.

 1787 Constitution
 +250 5 Jubilees of favor
 2037 End of age

 1776 U.S. Independence
 +239 1787 - 1776 = 11 years - 5 Jubilees (250)
 2015 UN subjugation

Could it be possible that the U.N.'s plan to subvert the U.S. Constitution is an ecological rouse? Is the real reason behind immigrants flooding across the southern border dictated by the 2015 U.N. mandate requiring nations to participate in these actions? Will the U.S. survive until 2037? Is this the reason for dismantling all historical statues across the country? Are they diluting the concepts of national citizenship in favor of world citizenship? Are they in favor of population control like China? Are pandemics ultimately used behind the scenes to ration food, water, and medical supplies? Production has been ramping down, blamed mostly on COVID-19 supply bottlenecks. But the truth of the matter reveals something more sinister. Mysterious delays, plant fires, and closings have plagued food U.S. food supplies which have largely gone unnoticed. United States farmers are being restricted by governmental regulation and from water rights. Without water, crops will cease. These shortages will enable pivotal leaders to seize total control and revisit the days of starvation ala Stalin and Mao. Communism is quietly famous for starving millions of their own citizens in the name of progress. Any mild hiccup will send shock waves through starving communities nationwide. For example, should a larger war erupt, this could be the spark that sets things ablaze. Perhaps the Nipah virus or a COVID-19 comeback would be the next catalyst. The kill rate for the Nipah virus is 40-75%. Surely the spirit realm sees the manifestation of events before any physical reflection. The powers of darkness are racing to prevent the advent of the coming Kingdom of God.

Let's revisit Noah's lifespan again. Notice how sandwiching the flood represented as 42 responds to identify Ishmael.

    1948   Israel nationhood
    + 19   1st set of Noah
    1967   Jerusalem reunited

    1967   Jerusalem reunited
    + 42   Antichrist number
    2009   Netanyahu's 2nd term & President 44

    2009   Israeli Prime Minister
    + 19   2nd set of Noah
    2028   Israeli Prime Minister 3rd term ends

Benjamin Netanyahu is currently serving his 3rd term as Israeli Prime Minister. His first stint extended through U.S. President 42, 1996-1999, the last Age of 6,000 years. He held the position of 13th Prime Minister and 9th person overall. His 2nd election encompassed U.S. President Ishmael plus 4 additional years. That Prime Minister's office number was 17th and 13th person overall. Netanyahu's 3rd term as Israeli Prime Minister will likely conclude by 2028-2029, as the 16th person to hold office as the 20th Israeli Prime Minster. This will complete 20-21 years of breakthrough service after his 3rd term. Benjamin means son of the right hand, emphasized by the Lord's number 3. Following these ministers, the opposition will assume the office of the 10th Secretary-General of the United Nations. Presently many Muslim countries have enough money to have enormous influence over such worldly decisions. Case in point, Abu Dhabi is a member of the U.N., an active NATO partner, and a member of the Istanbul Cooperation Initiative Framework. As a U.N. member, they have close ties with the World Bank. Abu Dhabi's substantial wealth spreads its influence across the oceans and into major financial markets. Colin Powers suggests that 2 Emirati sovereign-wealth funds invested inside the U.S. exceeded $800 billion in assets by 2020. Thus, a single Arab country is responsible for up to half the daily market volume. Some of their investments are handled by Blackrock, which manages approximately 10 trillion dollars in total assets. Blackrock is on record as pro-Palestinian and pro-Zoroastrian. If pressure is applied to put a Muslim at the helm of the U.N. it will happen. Israel's conflict with Hamas will be the focal point of this pressure. However, the appointment won't last. It is a means to an end, a flare over the bow for the wise.

Conflict within the Islamic religion can be vicious as well. Both sects often fight together but are just as quick to kill one another. For example, if Abu Dabhi and Saudi Arabia pushed for a Sunni leader in the role of Secretary-General of the United Nations it might quickly be viewed as provoking Iran into retaliatory reaction. As previously stated, Iran is predominately Shia. Since Iran remains the only Arab country pursuing nuclear weapons, once obtained they could opt to rapidly deploy that weapon against the leaders who pushed for Sunni representation. Some scholars believe Revelation depicts this event happening to the mysterious sister city of Babylon. Each book in the series gave clear reasons why this city is Mecca of Saudi Arabia. However, none of my books specifically calls for the destruction of Mecca. Rather, destruction of the abomination of desolation mentioned in scripture involves both Mount Moriah mosques. Whether purposefully or accidentally this specific destruction will occur by Muslim hands via armed combat or terrorism.

Herein lies the likely scenario to unfold. The Hamas war will soon incorporate the assistance of ISIS and Hezbollah to form their trinity. Turkey has expressed interest in giving aid to Hamas. Of course, Iran financially backs them all with money supplied through Ishmael. Turkey and Cypress have a long history with a final short stint to be fulfilled together. To make matters more volatile, since Turkey has expressed interest in aiding Hamas, Israel has lobbied against their membership in NATO. Under these parameters, Turkey may find it necessary to seek Russian backing and investigate joining BRIC partners, Brazil, Russia, India, and China, particularly if the rich Islamic oil nations join. Russia was the main instigator of the Suez Crises during the 1950's. At this juncture, the opposing players have expanded to a minimum of 5. Israel will likely be backed primarily by the United States, England, Italy, and Canada. This is the season the sun will set on Daniel's 10th Persian Empire. Satan and his final governments of socialism will be thrown into the lake of fire defeated. Left standing will be the 2 witnesses of Judaism and Christianity, the Old Testament and the New Testament. All those resisting reconciliation of one unified faith will bow down and be judged guilty. This is not the forced unification that this world order has to offer, but the choice of consolidation that splits the faith between the Gentile and the Jew. Revelation's healing leaves are meant for these.

The region of Turkey is rich in historical significance. Asian Minor incorporated the first 7 churches and witnessed the rise and fall of many early empires. Some mirrors have been discovered through these ages. Bible-prophecy.org lists 539

B.C. as the mirror of 539 A.D., each representing the fall of Babylon; 612 B.C. is the mirror of 612 A.D., the fall of Assyria. Thus, the sieges of Babylon and Assyria are numerically linked by 1150 years. This same mirror exists for empire cycles of 1260 years, 1290 years, 1335 years, and probably others. However, the interesting discovery rests within this mirror of 1335 years.

724-722 B.C.	Fall of Israel
-612-614 A.D.	Fall of Assyria
1335 years	Hamas mirror

You may have noticed that 722 B.C. is the mirror of 722 A.D., the fall of Israel. Thus, the sieges of Israel and Assyria are numerically linked. Therefore, it stands to reason that Israel's restoration might also be numerically linked. Could this latest conflict with Hamas be numerically linked? Let's investigate:

2023 A.D.	Israel Hamas War
-1335 years	Assyria gap
688 A.D.	Abomination of desolation

688 A.D.	Abomination of desolation
-1335 years	2nd gap for discovery
648 B.C.	Assyria defeats Babylon 3-year siege

Our math validates the context. The Hamas War is linked to the original Islamic mosque built in 688 A.D. and the Assyrian heritage of the 12 tribes of Ishmael as prescribed by Islam. And, if that same theme maintains continuity, the current war will last 2-3 years, until 2025-2026. Rosh Hashanah 2026 begins the Hebrew calendar year 2027. This year proposes another parallel alignment with the 1776 calculation concerning the United States. Will another treaty be signed only to blow up by 2030 or 2037?

Elohim is a God of order often discovered within the mathematical computations we aspire to uncover. In this vain, let's re-examine several items previously mentioned, starting with the feasts. What would it tell us if we deployed the feasts onto a mathematical chart? The data below lists the last 4 unfulfilled feasts, including Shemini Atzeret. Using the identical feast format of days for years we can begin with the politically identifiable date of Jerusalem becoming the recognized capital of Israel in 2017 A.D., give or take a year by measure of the Jewish calendar.

Event	Length	Year	Description
Yom Teruah	Day 1-2	2016-17	Capital coronation
Days of Awe	**10 days**	25-26	Repentance years
Yom Kippur 25 hour fast	1 day included	2025-2026	Elul prayer ends Elijah rises @ 51
Y = 10	1 day	26-27	**10 tests for Jews**
H = 5	7 days	27-28	Redemptive grace
W = 6	1 day	28-29	Adam binds Ismael
H = silent	4 days	29-30	The Law Books
Sukkot 3rd pilgrimage	7 days	36-37	Calculating sin Revelation 7 vials

| Shemini Atzeret | 1 day | 37-38 | 1st & 8th day return |

On December 6th, 2017, President Trump officially declared Jerusalem as the capital of Israel. This occurred during Chanukah otherwise known as Hanukkah. Hanukkah commemorates the rededication of the temple. This connection is undeniable. If we align this 2017 temple coronation with the 1st or 2nd day of Yom Teruah, Rosh Hashanah, each feast can be aligned with the remainder of time through 2037-2038. Notice the distance between 2017 and 2038 equals the same calculation as YHW(H). In Hebrew, the 2nd (H) is often silent. Could these 3 letters of the Almighty's name also represent the trinity? Remember, 4 represents the distance from heaven to earth, leading us to the breakthrough at Shemini Atzeret 2038 (H). Does this mimic the silence in heaven before Christ's resurrection at the 1st Trump as written in Seer in the Way? I believe these YHWH years are set aside and ordained for a special one-time purpose.

```
2038 A.D.     Shemini Atzeret
-2017 A.D.    Israel Hamas War
 21 years     Breakthrough

 10           Y
 + 5          H
 + 6          W
 21 years     Breakthrough
```

The Days of Awe span 10 years toward Yom Kippur and the 4 years of YHWH. These 10 years of judgment could represent the repayment of lost Jubilees from Rabbi Judah's prophecy and the mirror of the Egyptian plagues. All bear the scars of our deeds in life. Isaiah 53. Notice that the 4 days of YHWH fill the gap between Yom Kippur and Sukkot. This scenario mirrors Exodus 3 when YHWH appears to Moses declaring the purpose to rescue the elect. It also reflects the New

Testament idea of a rapture. Ostensibly, this quest has inadvertently tripped into confirming the window of the rapture. Just as the Magi knew the season of Christ's birth, we can approximate His return. But, if you will not wake up, Yeshua will come like a thief, Revelation 3:3.

All the data presented aligns with the probability of at least 1 significant church event before 2037-2038. Remember Rabbi Davidson's submission of 2028 as the Sabbatical date aligns with a possible rapture date. If so, now we can say that the Walls of Jericho have fallen a 2nd time. Will the final 7 years of Sukkot mirror a time of judgment just as Yeshua cleanses the temple for 7 days in Revelation 22? Jewish tradition suggests God calculates sin during Sukkot while the Hebrew is protected with "clouds of glory." As this festival is the last of 3 pilgrimages, it seems to reaffirm another return aiming to include the Jew after the final tribulation has begun. What does the beginning of tribulation look like? Are we already in it?

This last chart came 2 Saturday's (10 days) before the U.S. election #47 and suggests an overlap of the final 4 years of YHWH and the 2nd reign of Jehu. After 10 years of Awe notice the value of Gematria letters from J E H U equals 19. Could this be a reminder of the days of Noah? Watch the duplication to the same 2037-2038 end date.

21	YHWH
+ 19	Jehu
40	Years

1997	6,000
+ 40	Years
2037	Last year

Remember, Jehu always defeats the Jezebel representative. This implies the United States President of #45 also repeats as #47. Thus, it appears that Ephraim will defend Israel perhaps until the church is called home. However, that statement does not guarantee the completion of the entire 4-year presidency term. God could return any year. Yet, the more plausible spiritual explanation is the removal of God's grace before total destruction. One might consider this ordination reinforced by the Presidential nominee birth name, Daniel 2:21. The name Donald translates "World Ruler." Certainly, the United States is the lone superpower remaining. Only a collapse from within could defeat such a world dominant kingdom. Still, all kingdoms will come under the subjection of Christ, one way or another. Secondly, the old term Trump is synonymous with the modern meaning Trumpet. Together, Donald Trump may infer the sounding of the final 7th Trump followed by a church rapture. No doubt this proposition will unnerve many believers and political opponents. Regardless of human emotions, when God ordains any event, even a presidential election, all the forces of darkness will not prevail. It appears reasonable that the period of silence from seal #7 will be answered by Trumpet #7 as found in Revelation chapter 10.

YHWH Hebrew	JEHU Gematria	Presidential Term #47
Y = 10	J = 10	2025-2026
Heh = 5	E = 5	2026-2027
W = 6	H = 8	2027-2028

| H = Silent | U = 6 | 2028-2029 |

One of the stories in <u>Seer in the Way</u> speaks of a cruise in the Mediterranean. However, I didn't mention that it also marked the beginning of a reoccurring impression. Each time I boarded a cruise ship or a boat for the next 12 years, I periodically peered over the top floor railing across the open sea. I had come to love the salt air since my youth when mom moved us to that Atlantic Beach house rental. As a child, that salt air seemed to get clogged in my nasal passages but after getting used to the cleansing natural effects, I couldn't wait to inhale it again anytime we had been away. Anyway, the sensation that came to me periodically was that of a tidal wave. It was quite unnerving at times. I found myself constantly scanning the horizon as if to see something coming. It seemed at any moment a swell might materialize into a monstrous wall of water. While I was entirely certain something would happen, I was uncertain what or when it would happen. At that point, I wasn't completely convinced the vision was meant to be taken literally. Of course, tidal waves have occurred across the globe since then, but I never felt the nagging to keep up with those sorts of things. For years that feeling of a coming wave ebbed and flowed from time to time just enough to remind me that something had yet to arrive. Now I realize this was a warning of a looming financial tsunami.

In the immediate future, the financial strain of continuous war and overspending will cause a purposeful monetary collapse. Or perhaps, a huge number of missing people will dismantle supply and demand in the world's economy. Here is my latest dream that seems to infer this coming fate... Several banking members arrived at my doorstep to inform me that 2 relatives needed care. Apparently, the institution could no longer offer services. Realizing something was amiss, I agreed to follow several of them back to their local branch only to find the bank was vacant, completely cleaned out, void of a vault, furniture, countertops, carpet, etcetera. Approximately 2 dozen employees gather around to hear my assessment of the situation. It was understood that most of my relative's money had been surreptitiously spent. Thus, the reason for releasing tenants and closing the branch. The dream replayed in a loop a second time. I lay in a semi-awakened state to ask what it all meant. The best I can gather so far is that the first relative was Uncle Sam. The second relative seemed related to Uncle Sam though more distantly. Thus, the 2nd relative is likened to the Federal Reserve.

Since the bank was completely stripped of all previous improvements it implied bankruptcy or reorganization. Since my relatives, Uncle Sam and the Federal Reserve, were almost broke I was left with the sense that the banks were moving on or perhaps they expected the citizenry to bail them out. The employees waiting inside the vacant branch gathered around me for instructions almost as if they were beholden to me. What stood out to me was the thorough lack of remorse or responsibility they all exhibited for the mismanagement of funds. Truly these are the days in which we all live; days where no one takes accountability or weighs the consequences of their actions facilitated by the age of cart blanche victimhood. Surely a Sukkot Day of accountability is right around the corner, visible only to the customer who isn't morally bankrupt; visible only to the citizens who have not traded campaign contributions for contracts; visible only to those leaders and business owners who do not manipulate the masses with false truths and political agendas. Only 5 olive oil pilgrims will persevere beyond the reckoning of judgment day. The other half who pretend not to care will persecute the righteous and unrighteous alike, until their very last opportunity. That is the path they have chosen from the beginning, predestined. But God is just to have us convict ourselves, even by our own hands. Even the citizens of free countries trap themselves by casting their votes for the ungodly.

George Orwell's book 1984 foresaw a government that maintains control by surveillance. The computer age has surpassed that capability to the point of manipulating and directing control. Inevitably, this equates to zero control only noticeable after the wheels fall off. Computer companies like CrowdStrike exemplify this thesis as evidenced by the lawsuits yet to be filed for failing to maintain operational standards. Aldous Huxley's book The Brave New World takes a slightly different tact with the narrative that governments will keep citizens just happy enough to never revolt. This should sound familiar to the educated or to those who have paid attention to the political warnings within this book. This book endorses Orwell's and Huxley's views as true to some extent. Orwell went on to say, he feared book banning while Huxley hypothesized that no one would want to read. Sadly, both are true. Ironically, book banning centers largely against conservative views, and technology has encroached upon the commitment for educational learning. Besides, a socialist society is constantly at odds with educating the public, in any meaningful way. This explains the root problem with public education. It is a moral and ethical predicament of the heart embraced in a sea of apathy. The lazy nature of this society no longer reads because they don't value information. Orwell feared withholding of information while Huxley feared an overload of information. Again, both are true. Finally, Orwell figured hate would consume us and Huxley thought feelings and pleasures would ruin us. Once again, we have already arrived at both destinations at the same time.

In closing, what did Orwell and Huxley miss? McNamara's Morons. A study was performed in the United States Marine Corps. Essentially, rather than dismissing substandard privates they were disbursed into stronger units to reintegrate them. Those units that incorporated lower standards had substantially larger fatality rates. Yet, despite the proof and in the face of death, our society pushes a culture of diversity. Moving from a performance-based standard to any other criteria self-induces a virus or cancer that will rot a culture from the inside out. Clearly, the results have already been evident though perhaps surreptitiously ignored. Will civilization mandate itself to this cause until the very last man falls? McNamara's diversity study has exposed those who killed our troops, brought 200 billion dollars of central bank losses in one year, and killed citizens in the wake of natural disasters. By Shemini Atzeret, the 4th fall feast - and the 8th, all Satanic ideologies will be "cut off" like a lake is unto a river. Those regimes will join the false prophet or image previously captured in 1967. All else embracing falsities will be eternally thirsty. In the meantime, why not receive the special blessing offered by studying the book of Revelation? The church's hard-core hands-off approach will deny many believers that opportunity. Everyone will be accountable in the end.

Isaiah 61

2 Peter 1:12-13

Made in the USA
Columbia, SC
16 November 2024